D1367400

Transform Your Company for the Innovation Universe

Acclaim for
Transform Your Company for the Innovation Universe

A guided tour of the "innovation universe" by a wise practitioner/teacher who created this comprehensive and accessible framework for those who desire to become more accomplished innovators within their own organizations.

Harry L. Davis,
Roger L. and Rachel M. Goetz Distinguished Service Professor of Creative Management, The University of Chicago Booth School of Business

Transform Your Company for the Innovation Universe provides a practical framework that was built from Nancy's twenty-plus-year journey of innovation. Nancy is a perpetual learner who has taken a framework that she helped develop during her time at Whirlpool and then evolved this framework based on insights provided by literally thousands of business leaders, educators, and, most importantly, innovation practitioners. The result is a must-read for every innovation practitioner.

Michael McDonnell,
Chief Technology and Innovation Officer, Amsted Rail, Amsted Industries

I met Nancy during a conference years ago. She inspired me because she was speaking to a room filled with people and at the same time it felt like she was speaking to me personally. She has been inspiring me ever since, and with this book, she is doing it again. This book gives practitioners the understanding of how to make innovation part of a company's DNA.

Angelique Plugge,
Innovation Driver, ING

While many have written on the topic, few reveal the practical insights necessary to drive innovation forward within an organization. Now one of the strongest voices shares her proven skills and knowledge in a highly insightful and engaging read—finally, a playbook for innovation practitioners.

Adam Bowen,
Senior Vice President, Group Strategic Planning Director, FCB

Along with Beacon's long heritage of innovation, Nancy's Insights helped focus and clarify our innovation intent and investment. Nancy's decades-long perspective allowed Beacon to accelerate work on behalf of our customer."

Lori Turner,
Chief Marketing, Innovation and Experience Officer, Beacon Health System

Also, By Nancy A. Tennant

Unleashing Innovation, Tennant Snyder and Duarte

Strategic Innovation, Tennant Snyder and Duarte

Mastering Virtual Teams, Duarte and Tennant Snyder

Transform Your Company for the Innovation Universe

FRAME | GENERATE | EMBED | LEAD

Nancy A. Tennant

Moonfish
PRESS

Published by Moonfish Press
innovationuniverse.com

Readers should be aware that Internet sites offered as citations or sources for further information may have changed or disappeared between the time this was written and when it is read.

Disclosure: The author is associated with the University of Chicago and the University of Notre Dame as a paid instructor. No other endorsements or financial associations exist between the author and suggested websites, authors, or references.

Library of Congress Cataloging-in-Publication Data
Tennant, Nancy, 2019.
Transform Your Company for the Innovation Universe: Frame. Generate. Embed. Lead. /Nancy Tennant
    Includes bibliographic references and index.
    ISBN 13: 978-1-7328415-0-5 - (paperback)
    ISBN 13: 978-1-7328415-1-2 (e-book)
    ISBN 978-1-7328415-2-9 (hardback)
    LCCN: 2018914011
    1. Innovation. 2. Embed. 3. Culture Change. 4. Organization change. 5. Leadership. 6. Strategy. 7. Transformation

First Edition: February 2019

To my aunt,
Dr. Anita Harbert,
luminary and illuminatus

Rumored to be the
matriarch of the
Raspa/Simonetti illuminati

CONTENTS

Preface

The matter, energy, and force of your Innovation Universe are,
as yet, unknown.

Over twenty years ago, the chairman and CEO of Whirlpool Corporation called me into his office and asked me to lead the inaugural innovation effort at the organization. He said he wanted innovation from everywhere and everyone and that if we are successful, every job in the company will change. I nodded in agreement as he spoke, but my internal voice was saying: we both speak the same language, but I have no idea what you are asking me to do.

At the time, innovation inside companies, including Whirlpool, was not how we think of it today. At best, it was good product development. If you picked up a business journal, the cover story might be about a twenty-something overnight millionaire in Silicon Valley who founded the dot-com of the moment. Over his (and it would always be a male) head on the cover was a title along the lines of "The New Innovators." If you were a "bricks and mortar" company, this world was as far away from you as it could possibly be. There were very few models for how to transform your company to be innovative from the inside out.

We tend to forget how new innovation really is in the annals of management science. Luckily, many practitioners, entrepreneurs, academics, and consultants have helped define innovation as we now know it. Many large companies have been practicing innovation for many years and working to get their innovation initiatives to the next level. Yet every day, companies of all sizes in all industries are just starting on their own innovation journey.

Innovation practitioners

In those early years of innovation, what sparked my passion was that innovation was migrating out of the Valley and into companies. With that migration, innovation was retooled for the masses. No longer did you have to be a garage genius to try it. Given the right framing, training, support, and resources, diverse teams within companies could innovate. What the CEO was asking me to do was to democratize innovation and embed it as a core competency in the company. It was never about lighting a million fires; it was about embedding innovation as a strategic driver of organic growth.

As I traveled along my own innovation journey, I began to see the unique value in the practitioner's view of the domain. Informed by innovation thought leaders, celebrity academics, and big-name consulting firms, companies across the spectrum of industries charged internal practitioners with embedding innovation. The key to their success was, and still is, transforming the company and equipping employees to become innovators. But how?

Innovation practitioners' stories are hardly ever heralded. Innovation practitioners are those who work for organizations and are actively engaged in leading or influencing an innovation initiative. Many innovation practitioners remain behind the scenes, making the innovation initiative work but not taking credit. They enjoy the success and endure the failure in relative isolation. Yet, it takes practitioners at every level in a company to start and sustain innovation:

- **Senior leaders** who create the environment and establish a North Star for innovation.
- **Innovation leads,** Chief Innovation Officers, or VPs of Innovation who create the blueprint and remove barriers at the enterprise level.
- **Innovation teams** on the front lines who create and deliver solutions to create value for their customers.
- **Everyday business leaders** who embed innovation in their practice areas.
- **Facilitators** of innovation who mentor and assist innovation teams as they navigate the transition from idea development to commercialization.

Thought leaders, academics, and consultants create many of the theories and tools to teach and enable innovation, but it is you—the practitioner—who makes innovation work in companies.

Who should read this book and why?

There are very few books that offer a practitioner's perspective on how to transform companies to become innovation powerhouses. Even fewer take the amorphous topic of innovation and simplify it so that all companies can apply the ideas. It's hard for practitioners to make sense of the dizzying array of branded innovation theories and models available today. The Innovation Universe[1], presented in this book, offers a framework designed specifically for innovation practitioners to use as they launch, improve, and evolve their company's innovation initiative. If your company has charged you with leading an innovation initiative, as mine once did, or if you are leading innovation teams, you can use the ideas and solutions in this book to take innovation to the next level. If you teach corporate innovation in business schools, this book is a resource to help your students understand how to systemically transform a company to be more innovative. If you teach innovation workshops to practitioners, this book can serve as a companion to your interactive content.

This volume is part business book and part memoir. I am lucky to be a longtime innovator with a rich and exciting innovation career. I continue to work with the most interesting organizations and dynamic people in the innovation space.

In my workshops, participants ask about my experiences as a practitioner and longtime innovation advisor. They enjoy my candor and success stories, and they learn from the mistakes I made along the way. This book brings these stories together with a proven framework for making innovation a core competency within organizations. I teach this framework to practitioners and put it into practice in companies of all shapes and sizes. What I have found is that this framework for delivering innovation within organizations adds value because it is carefully designed to meet the needs of practitioners. It offers a clear path to embed innovation as a core competency without derailing the everyday operations you need to succeed.

Why me?

I know what it is like to be on the front lines of innovation. I led the charge at Whirlpool Corporation for close to twenty years.

We started at the dawn of the field in the late 1990s, when it was new territory to everyone, including my colleagues and myself. During that time, I grappled with innovation along with a host of gifted and dedicated people. All of us were trying to turn Whirlpool into a company that put the customer at the center of everything, offering innovative solutions to their problems. It was an incredible experience for me as a practitioner; those years at Whirlpool had a profound impact on my thinking and offered a multitude of learnings that I carry with me today.

To broaden my perspective and continue learning, I teach innovation at two of the world's leading business schools, the University of Chicago and the University of Notre Dame. As part of that work, I teach and interact with thousands of executives from hundreds of companies that are trying to make their organizations more competitive through innovation.

Over time, I've learned that teaching and writing are themselves innovations, no less demanding and creative than any commercial endeavor. As such, I've cowritten three books, including *Unleashing Innovation: How Whirlpool Transformed an Industry*, which has become required reading for MBAs, including those at Harvard Business School.[2]

In other words, not only have I paid my dues as a founding member of the innovation movement, but I also continue to evolve and grow as I work with practitioners on the front lines today.

Since I started working in innovation, the space has exploded. Still, innovation is far from a systemized, codified approach, the way quality or customer relationships became core business processes. Until that time, which I believe is several years away, take heart, for we are all learning and discovering innovation together.

One of the CEOs at Whirlpool had a saying that I think sums it up nicely. Each time we looked at how far the company had come with innovation, he said, "We are perpetually dissatisfied." For those of you who did not grow up in the midwestern United

States, allow me to translate. Innovation is a continuous improvement endeavor. Those who engage in it are always accumulating knowledge and taking innovation to the next level.

In some ways, this makes it nice for those of you who are coming into innovation now. There is no one company, one consultancy, or one expert source that has it all figured out. Innovation is constantly evolving and advancing.

This book is about how you can evolve and advance your organization from the inside out, adapting it to be more innovative. A young man in one of my MBA classes, after absorbing and experiencing the Innovation Universe in the workshop, said to me: "You can use this framework for any kind of enterprise transformation." I agree. That's one way to think about this book, as a guide to organizational transformation with innovation as its central muse.

Getting the most out of this book

The Innovation Universe is an open-source framework. I created it by synthesizing hundreds, if not thousands, of insights, nuggets, processes, tools, and frameworks that I tested in my innovation profession. It is more of a flexible organizing framework than a static theory. The Innovation Universe helps you organize your thinking so that you can establish a baseline of understanding about innovation and then build on that to grow your knowledge—and your innovation initiative—as you build tools and gain experience.

The core chapters in this book explain, deconstruct, and help you put the Innovation Universe framework into practice in your organization. We will examine each of the foundations in the framework in detail, and I will illustrate how they work using stories and examples.

Interspersed throughout this book, along with a great deal of implementation advice and expert guidance, is a unique feature that I call Innovation Pivots. These are depictions of the lighter side of innovation within organizations. I would argue that you won't make it as an innovator without a sense of humor. I hope these Innovation Pivots provide emotional support to sustain you on your innovation journey. If they make you laugh or smile, pass them along to your colleagues.

Learn More

There are also ancillary resources that can advance your understanding of the Innovation Universe once you've read and earmarked this book. And, as mentioned, I coauthored several books and articles on innovation.

You can learn about all of these resources and others on my website, *innovationuniverse.com.* You can also dive deeper into the Innovation Universe through the Innovation Universe Masterclass Series, an online series of workshops I created to help practitioners learn more about the Innovation Universe, at *https://innovation-universe-series.thinkific.com/collections.*

You can explore the workshops I offer at the University of Notre Dame by visiting *https://innovationacademy.nd.edu.*

CHAPTER 1

The Innovation Universe

The Innovation Universe consists not of individual stars, but of constellations of everyday dreamers.

A joke I know goes like this: a tourist is lost in Ireland. Frustrated, she stops to ask one of the Irish locals for directions to Dublin. "Ok," he says, "I'll give you directions, but if I were you, I certainly wouldn't start from here."

I sometimes think this joke describes what happens when leaders go looking for models and guides to make their company more innovative. There are precious few resources in the marketplace that help companies start from where they are, and acknowledge that they, not an outside entity, are best equipped to lead their innovation initiative.

Instead, the market is more apt to push the latest fads, tools, or cookie-cutter approaches to innovation. Doesn't it seem odd that innovation, of all things, is becoming a copycat industry? To make matters worse, some consultants insist that you invest in their proprietary approach or latest app, whether it's right for your company or not.

But innovation is a combination of art and science that each company must lead for itself, starting with the traits and assets that make that company unique. And it *can* be done: Your company can create a scalable innovation approach that complements your strategy. Your innovation initiative can grow and adapt as your organization grows and adapts. Your company can describe an innovation sandbox: a target for innovation that invites all employees and partners to create innovations from everywhere and everyone.

Think about it this way: innovation should be a core competency in a company, not an outsourced skill. That's where the Innovation Universe comes in.

CATS AND INNOVATION

1. Both play with your mind.
2. The key is don't get too attached.
3. When you want them most, they both elude you.
4. Both are indifferent to your effort.
5. Cheap tools can distract them.

Innovation Pivot 1.

Welcome to the Innovation Universe

The Innovation Universe is a unifying framework for companies that want to embed innovation into their DNA. I created it after years of leading innovation at Whirlpool Corporation[3] and subsequently working with many other organizations to create a path for systemic innovation. I've used these varied experiences to develop and generalize insights about innovation from a variety of companies. In the process, I tested these insights in numerous settings to see what held true across industries and organization type and size. Over time, I came to realize that it was possible to create a common framework for innovation.

The Innovation Universe framework provides an expanse of innovation knowledge, to help companies create and improve customized innovation initiatives. It offers an approach that makes innovation an organizational competency. And it forges a path that your organization can follow to allow innovation to thrive year after year, flowing across the divide of business units, hierarchies, and job titles.

NASA created a vast resource called the Cosmicopia. Its website states that "Cosmicopia contains an abundance (a cornucopia) of information about cosmic rays, the Earth's magnetosphere, the Sun, space weather, and other exciting topics on space science."[4] With NASA's Cosmicopia as one inspiration (celestial guidance, if you will) for the Innovation Universe, this book creates the first "innovation Cosmicopia." Innovation Universe is a simplified description, a collection of powerful resources, and a practical framework for companies that want to begin or accelerate their innovation efforts.

More specifically, the Innovation Universe framework provides innovation leaders with essential information and options to start or improve their innovation initiative. It does not prescribe any one path; instead, it offers a menu of generalized and normative actions for you to consider as you lead and operationalize your company's innovation effort. The Innovation Universe puts you in control by providing a framework to help your team select, alter, or reject innovative ideas and approaches from other companies, consultants, workshops, books, and academics. The Innovation Universe framework is simple to understand but not necessarily easy to implement, depending on your organizational barriers and existing norms. Even so, it will give you a reliable reference point—celestial guidance—as you sample innovation approaches, tools, and insights. What makes the Innovation Universe unique and valuable is that it:

- Provides a diagnosis and simplifies the systems and behaviors within your company.
- Allows you to transform only the specific aspects of your company required for innovation.
- "Plays nicely" with other key initiatives such as operational excellence, six sigma and lean.
- Targets the highest-leveraged areas of your overall strategy.
- Helps you scale innovation as you lead it to the next level.

The Innovation Universe 4x4 matrix

If you could rocket out into space and look back at your company with perspective, using an Innovation Universe lens, you will see a universal and practical view that many companies share. In the Innovation Universe, innovation is:

> GENERATING + delivering a cadence of unique + value-creating solutions for customers, while FRAMING + LEADING innovation as a core competency, EMBEDDED in every aspect of your company.

In the Innovation Universe, the innovation space looks organized and orderly, with four distinct foundations. The framework describes the observable space and matter that every company should consider when embedding innovation. Innovation paths come into focus and connections become clearer. In essence, it offers a view from space to help you understand the big picture of innovation and where your company can position itself to begin or to accelerate its unique innovation journey.

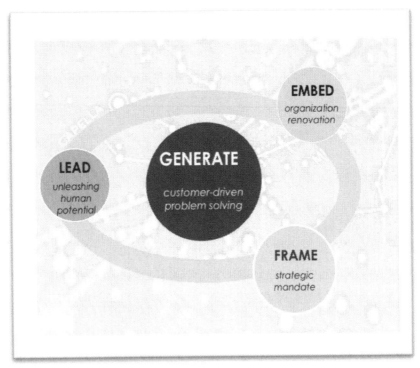

Figure 1. The Innovation Universe.

Unlike any other universe, the Innovation Universe has a sun and three orbiting planets that are the *foundations* of the universe. Foundations are determinants that contribute to an outcome, in this case transforming your company to be more innovative. The four foundations of the Innovation Universe are FRAME, GENERATE, EMBED, and LEAD.

If you drill down into each foundation, you will find a myriad of *elements* that can help your company be more innovative. Based on my experiences and the many hours I spend with companies and innovation practitioners, I selected elements that represent what I consider the most pressing opportunities or decisions for companies that are transforming themselves for greater innovation. If you want to see a concise summary of the four foundations, jump to Table 9 at the end of the book.

The GENERATE foundation is the art and science of creating innovations, from concept to commercialization. As such, it is the center of the Innovation Universe. Many companies start and stop at GENERATE. To the keen observer, there are three additional foundations that orbit GENERATE and complete the Innovation Universe: FRAME, EMBED, and LEAD. The FRAME foundation is how you set the stage for innovation and enable strategy execution. The EMBED foundation is how you renovate your company to make innovation thrive over time. More than just culture, EMBED creates change in hard-edged elements of the organization as well, like systems and processes. LEAD is how you, as a leader, can unleash human potential in yourself and others as active participants in the innovation economy. Each of these four foundations is wide-ranging enough to hold the critical know-how required to renovate your company for the innovation age. Everything you are doing or will do in innovation can find a place on one of the four foundations of understanding.

Innovation Pivot 2.

Before we explore each of the four foundations in the Innovation Universe, we need to put on lenses that bring the entire Innovation Universe into proper focus. The first lens looks at how organizations view their ability to innovate in the Innovation Universe by looking at nature vs. nurture. The second lens sees innovation as an always-on core competency. The third lens helps us balance innovation evolution and revolution. The fourth lens considers the paradox of discretion versus obligation.

The first lens: Balancing nurture and nature

It took me a lot longer than it should have to realize that in any C-suite there are two schools of thought about innovation. The first school—let's call it *nature*—believes that there are very bright people in the world who instinctively know how to innovate new products, services, and businesses. After all, that's the reason you hired them, right? These are the people you find running new business development, the ideation garage, the innovation lab, and often the strategy group. The second school of C-suite thought—call it *nurture*—believes that everyone can learn to innovate, especially when companies provide the appropriate resources, opportunities, and training.

Unfortunately, there is rarely a balcony view of nature and nurture, and the playing field view becomes an either/or battleground. To hedge your bets, you want both nature and nurture—sort of a bilateral accord where both views exist side by side.

I was recently at a large gathering of over six hundred innovation professionals representing more than 250 medium to large global companies. More than half of these companies were not yet at the point of understanding the "and" part of the bilateral accord; many were just getting started on their innovation journey. For the companies that *were* mature enough in their innovation initiative to create a bilateral agreement, a few positioned nature and nurture like this:

- **NATURE.** Aligned with disruptive new business models: seen often in start-ups/new business development groups in which innovation skills are already resident in hand-picked leaders and teams.

- **NURTURE.** Aligned with core incremental innovation: where employees are trained to be innovators.

This split approach is one viable option. The key is to realize that both views exist within every company, and you need to evolve to a point where you can sustain both.

Another approach for detente is the one-two punch. In this case, companies might start with *nature* in the form of a garage, incubator, or a new business development group, where they hire the team from the outside, but they don't train potential innovators from within their company. After a period, they realize that they have created an "in-group" of innovators, excluding virtually everyone else. In time, they move to a *nurture* phase, where they begin to equip and enable more and more employees to innovate.

Similarly, I worked with a large company that did this in reverse. The company started with innovation from everyone, and once they built the innovation muscle in everyday work, they set their sights on new business development, start-ups, and innovation garages. As with every aspect of innovation, what works for your company is determined by your business, culture, strategy, and innovation reach.

Which school of thought—nature or nurture—is more in line with creating innovation as a core competency within the Innovation Universe? The answer is *nurture*. Enabling sustainable innovation from everywhere and everyone requires an organizational environment that is intentional as opposed to fatalistic.

For the sake of illustration, let's liken the nurture perspective to becoming an elite runner. If you are a marathoner, you may have a *natural* ability to run. However, if you want to claim an edge, there are skills you can *nurture* to become more competitive. These skills include running schedules, nutrition, running psychology, and weight training. You could nurture any of these skills to become the basis of your personal competency as a runner, thereby adding an edge to your natural running ability.

The second lens: Innovation as a core competency

Organizational core competencies are indicative of the deep expertise that enables your company to deliver a type of value that is hard for your competitors to duplicate. Gary Hamel and C.

K. Prahalad first introduced the idea to companies in the 1990s. They likened organizations to trees and core competencies to the root system. Importantly, core competencies can be either resident or created—but they always need to be protected. They are often "invisible to the people who aren't deliberately looking for [them].[5] Hamel and Prahalad identified three tests of core competencies. They must:

- Provide access to new markets.
- Make a significant contribution to customer value.
- Be difficult for competitors to copy.

Core competencies are embedded organizational skills and assets that do not diminish with use. They can be optimized and scaled. Pretend again that you're a marathoner—your knee cartilage (*nature*) may diminish over time, but your potential to apply new skills to racing (*nurture*), which compensates for cartilage loss, will not. In the Innovation Universe, innovation as a core competency is:

- The glue that binds the core business.
- The engine for innovations in the core and beyond.
- Built around a continuous improvement process that may take years to optimize.
- Manifested in people and management systems.

The notion of a core competency is relevant to many of the Innovation Universe foundations. Core competencies play into how you FRAME innovation as part of your larger strategic mandate. They also should inform how you GENERATE innovations to solve problems and create opportunities for customers. You will find evidence of sustaining core competencies in the choices your company makes in EMBED. In addition, Innovation Universe LEADers should see their role as building and protecting innovation as a core competency, if one does not exist already. While innovation garages, incubators, or labs are in vogue, they are not enough. To be sustainable, innovation must exist throughout the organization and must migrate to the highest leveraged decisions that are critical to executing your strategy. To move beyond innovation as a set of disparate projects, or fires lit here and there, innovation must be developed and embedded as a core competency, thereby increasing the chance that it will be sustainable.

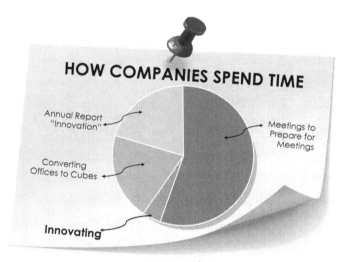

Innovation Pivot 3.

The third lens: Balancing evolution and revolution

There is nothing like innovation in the annals of management science. The uniqueness centers on its *revolutionary* nature, to which people are attracted. Innovation encourages breaking mental frames and seeing problems through new eyes. Yet, the *evolutionary* aspect of innovation is also relevant to the Innovation Universe, because that is how innovation is embedded in mature organizations—through an evolutionary and deliberate approach.

Another way to understand the revolutionary and evolutionary paradox is to consider that solving customer problems occupies two sides of a coin: one side is evolutionary through technical problem solving and continuous improvement, and the other side is revolutionary, through the adaptive problem solving offered by innovation.[6]

Evolution-deductive methodologies

Generally speaking, most of the management initiatives that companies have "hired" over the last two decades have been on the evolutionary side of the coin. These include lean, operational excellence, cost management, work-flow rationalization, delayering, Six Sigma, product quality, and reengineering, to name a few. In short, all of these reduce existing processes from the large to the granular level and then make changes to the ratio of input to output to improve efficiency, speed, and quality. As a generalization, evolutionary processes rely on standardized rules to solve specific problems. The mantra here is you can create value through continuous improvement. Evolutionary methodologies are vital for companies to survive.

Revolution-inductive methodologies

While the revolutionary perspective is also about solving problems, here we use skills sets and methodologies that are inductive and adaptive. Innovation fits squarely in the space, and often is the only inductive and adaptive management science you can find in companies. In revolutionary methodologies, you create the rules as the solution evolves. The mantra here is to ideate the most significant customer-centric value proposition to create a unique solution. In this case, the status quo needs to be over-turned (revolution), and you create value by bringing customers solutions (often groundbreaking) that entail new business models to offer value that no one else can provide. We know that revolutionary methodologies, of which innovation is the best example, are also vital for companies to survive.

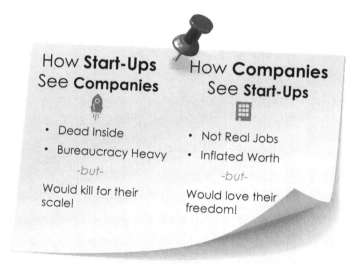

Innovation Pivot 4.

The fourth lens: The discretionary riddle

Close your eyes and imagine that everyone in your company is no longer an employee on your payroll but an unpaid volunteer. I know what you are thinking; this is the best cost-saving idea in the history of zero-based budgeting. It's not long before you re-alize that you will have to get tasks accomplished with people who don't have to comply and sing the company song. Volunteers have the discretion to show up or not. They vote with their feet concerning the types of tasks they take on and the roles they want to play. Now you are thinking, this is a nightmare.

One aspect that makes innovation unique is that, for the most part, it is discretionary. You arrive at work on Monday morning and you see an email with this subject line: Revised Budgets Due. You read the email and learn that your business unit is going to have to cut costs by 10 percent and that your revised budget is due at the end of the day. You may not like it, but you comply. Suppose, on the other hand, the subject line states:

New Breakthrough Ideas Due Friday. Maybe, maybe not.

Real innovation is discretionary—you want to do it; you are at-tracted to it. In its purest sense, innovation is a calling, not a forced march. In the Innovation Universe, leaders learn how to attract people to innovation. They learn how to honor and sup-port the creativity and the personal risk that it takes for employ-ees to innovate. Innovation can't be mandatory. Innovation from everyone and everywhere does not mean that on Friday in your company everyone must submit an idea. Rather, you will create an environment that attracts people to bring their best ideas for-ward and collaborate with others to bring innovations to market. The Innovation Universe will offer you some ideas on how to move from a compliance to an attraction model that unleashes innovation in your company.

Innovation Universe *takeaways*

Innovation is not necessarily linear, but the galaxy of the Innovation Universe can help make it more orderly and help organize your innovation initiative. As you progress in innovation over many years, you will proceed into deeper and more sophisticated aspects of innovation. The Innovation Universe framework has the elasticity to guide you to new levels. It provides an understanding of what you need to do and offers the tools and advice needed to take the first step, and every step after that.

In the Innovation Universe, innovation is defined as

> **Generating** and delivering a cadence of unique and value-creating solutions for customers, while **framing** and **leading** innovation as a core competency, **embedded** in every aspect of your company.

The Innovation Universe has four foundations to get your company's innovation initiative started or take it to the next level:

- FRAME is linking innovation to your strategy. GENERATE is the creation of innovations, from insights to commercialization. EMBED is changing the company to make innovation work for the long term. LEAD is adopting new skills and traits to allow innovations to thrive.

- Innovation occurs via nature and nurture. However, the Innovation Universe focuses on nurturing innovation to create and sustain it as a core competency.

- Innovation is a core competency, not a set of projects. It can become part of your company's DNA.

- Innovation is revolutionary and evolutionary. There is room for both in the Innovation Universe. We use revolutionary insights to bring new innovations to market while we prioritize evolution as a way to embed innovation in the company.

- Innovation is discretionary. It is not about asking everyone to submit ideas. Instead it is about creating the right environment to attract and support employees to become innovators and to bring their best ideas forward.

Chapter 1 | The innovation universe

CHAPTER 2

FRAME
The strategic mandate

*Teach a leader to FRAME and she will unleash innovation
from everywhere and everyone.*

I have a confession to make. When I first formulated the Innovation Universe framework, I did not include FRAME. I assumed most companies would automatically rationalize how innovation fit within their enterprise strategy. It was a naïve assumption. I remember being in a friendly debate with the head of an executive education department at one of the world's leading universities where I was delivering a guest lecture. As I described the framework, he said, "You are missing something: strategy." At the time I rejected his idea, not realizing how right he was until much later.

Truth be told, there is a fatal attraction common to innovation. Companies and their leaders get so charged up about generating new ideas that they set up teams and launch innovations posthaste. Unfortunately, in doing so they embed a fatal flaw into their innovation initiative. Leaders forget that their primary function in bringing innovations to market is not as the idea person, or the network liaison, or the mentor on a series of innovation teams, although these are all essential roles. The single most critical responsibility that leaders have within companies trying to bring innovations to market is creating and adapting an environment where innovation can thrive. Bypassing the less glamorous, heavy-lifting phase of connecting innovation to your strategy and speeding into innovation will not serve your innovation initiative well; in fact, it may derail it.

Testing your company's FRAME

Let me make the case using you as a sample size of one. Answer this series of questions about your company:

1. *Does your company have an enterprise strategy that includes vision, mission, strategies, values, and goals? (Extra points if that strategy positions innovation to drive value.)*

2. *Is your strategic architecture tangible and located all in one place? (If you had to present it in a court of law as "evidence," could you hold it up, physically or electronically, to submit it to the court?)*

3. *Is your strategic architecture accessible and available to all employees and is it understandable and (extra points here) inspiring?*

4. *Do the people who populate your innovation teams, both internal employees and external partners, understand and use your strategic architecture as a*

"sandbox" to collaborate, drive innovation efforts, and enable decision making?

5. *Do innovators reference the strategic architecture in their elevator pitch to get funding and other resources?*

The fatal attraction I mentioned often prevents us from seeing that there are "non-innovation" steps required for success in the innovation space. If you answered no to any of the questions above, your company needs to spend some time on the FRAME foundation of the Innovation Universe. Each question tests the strength of your innovation backstory and helps set the stage for innovation to enable strategy execution.

Question 1 is the essential backstory for innovation: Strategy formulation and senior leader alignment. In my executive education workshops, I begin the FRAME discussion by asking a simple question: *Raise your hand if your company has a strategic architecture.* About one-quarter of the participants raise their hands. More often, companies deploy innovation without an enterprise strategy that guides innovators' decisions and actions.

Question 2 is about knowing that you have something, but not being able to find it. Have you ever been traveling and realized you forgot your phone charger? You search everywhere. You empty your suitcase, briefcase, and purse. No luck. You make do by borrowing from someone who's come prepared. When you get home and unpack your suitcase, you discover the charger was there all along. Not to be overly existential, but if you have something yet can't put your hands on it, do you really have it? Here is how this problem plays out within companies:

- Only a few senior leaders have access to the strategy.
- The strategy is fragmented and found in several different departments.
- The strategy is in a presentation deck or Excel spreadsheet, not in a story that everyone tells.
- The key objectives are locked in a secure online dashboard.
- The strategies for each business unit require a phone call to the strategy lead (answered only if caller ID shows the call coming from the C-suite).
- The company goals are contained in a spreadsheet in the CFO's office.

In other words, if an innovator wants to see her company's strategic architecture, it takes a scavenger hunt to piece it together. The strategy does exist, it's just not "evidential."

Question 3 points to a backstory where strategy and innovation are not only linked but are also easy to understand and relate to individual roles and accountabilities. Companies that are known to be great innovators make sure every employee knows the strategy and can connect it to their work. An across-the-board understanding of the strategy by employees is not easy to achieve. It takes a great deal of constancy of purpose, overcommunication, repetition, and education, but it is essential to innovation.

Questions 4 and 5 are specific to innovation teams. If your teams are not starting their ideation efforts from a strategy sandbox (that is, a target, bounded by your strategy, where they can collaborate, experiment, and build on other people's ideas), then you are at risk of wasting scarce resources and frustrating potential innovators. Innovation teams need the strategic sandbox describing the areas where your company wants to place bets so that they know where to begin.

In my experience, successful innovation requires a positive response to all of these questions. The good news is that omissions and shortcomings can be addressed. They do not require new-to-the-world solutions—we have knowledge and best practices at the ready. The solution may prove as straightforward as creating a few new steps and assigning people in your company to ensure that:

- The strategic architecture is resident in your innovation backstory.
- Every employee understands the backstory in reference to his or her own role.
- All innovation occurs in lockstep with strategy execution.

FRAME is innovation's North Star

I recently worked with an international food company that was a market leader for over fifty years. More recently, however, it was experiencing a rapid loss in market share due to new competitive pressures and customer demands. Astutely, the firm decided it needed innovation to address this threat.

At the annual senior leadership conference, attendees discussed how to move forward. During the conference, I asked the senior leaders: Does your strategy address your customer's unmet needs, and how will innovation address these needs?

There was a pregnant pause and then a sound that was more like an orchestra tuning their instruments than a concert in progress. Everyone shouted out their thoughts on how to meet customer needs, but there was no harmony in how they would do it. It was a room full of incongruent ideas and opinions. When I asked them to describe how their strategy could guide their attempts to innovate, it was more of the same. Lots of ideas and opinions, but little alignment around their strategy or how to address customer needs. It was eye-opening for all of us.

As this scene unfolded, the company's new VP of Innovation, charged with leading the innovation initiative, and new Innovation Scout, who was seeking technology partners for future innovations, both sat in the front of the room observing the discord. They had already started launching teams and developing innovations. In this state of misalignment, it became clear to all of us that their innovation teams had little idea where to focus their efforts. It was a free-for-all. This is not a poorly run company; rather, it is a very well run and admired global organization.

This story corroborates an alarming data point I read recently in an excellent innovation research report by Pricewaterhouse-Coopers.[7] The 2017 report states that 54 percent of the companies surveyed were having a hard time linking innovation and business strategy. *More than half?*

This is where FRAME comes in.

FRAME is the North Star of the Innovation Universe. It will guide your overall innovation effort and orient your individual innovation projects by focusing innovation on areas that offer the highest value for your customers and your company. In every innovation workshop I host, I use FRAME as a conversation starter and a guardrail to help leaders understand their role in creating and organizing the backstory for innovation.

By definition, FRAME is:

> A clear and understood enterprise or business-unit strategy that requires innovation and includes why, who, where, how much, and when as well as the linkages and benefits from innovation for the company and its customers.

As we explore the other three foundations associated with the Innovation Universe, GENERATE, EMBED, and LEAD, we see that FRAME has an essential relationship with each. For example, as your organization launches innovations, FRAME and GENERATE will form a virtuous cycle. Specifically, as innovators interact with customers, observe results in the marketplace, and collect learnings, the GENERATE findings will inform your next strategy cycle within FRAME. Therefore, it is important that FRAME not become commingled, recede, or take a back seat to GENERATE—even when the innovation cycle is in its later stages. Fortunately, the Innovation Universe framework helps you separate these foundations and pause long enough to make the adjustments necessary so that GENERATE and FRAME can reinforce each other and increase value for your company.

FRAME and EMBED, as well, enjoy a critical and symbiotic relationship. EMBED guides the organizational changes required to make innovation succeed. EMBED has a core focus on adapting both management systems (hard side) and culture (soft side) so that innovation is sustainable. FRAME guides these organizational changes so that you adjust only what is required to make innovation work, while not eliminating aspects of your company that make it great.

Finally, FRAME and LEAD are interconnected as well. For instance, FRAME guides leaders in your company to develop the strategy and communicate it to all employees. Additionally, FRAME helps leaders use collaborative and iterative approaches to FRAME opportunities so that innovators can succeed. Again, the essential efforts on the FRAME foundation allow leaders to do their work better and take the lead in re-envisioning innovation during follow-up strategy cycles.

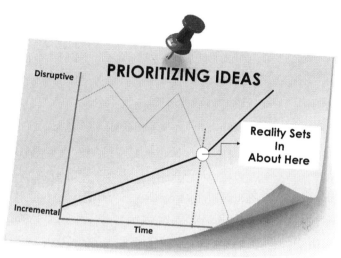

Innovation Pivot 5.

The four elements of FRAME

Each foundation has four elements to guide companies as they conceive and organize their innovation initiative. Within these elements, each offers a set of decisions to help leaders keep their innovation efforts on track for success. There are no mandates. Depending upon where you are in your innovation effort, and relative to your company's unique objectives, the Innovation Universe provides a menu of actions from which to choose. The four elements of FRAME are *strategic architecture, iBlueprint, definition + criteria*, and *structure + fit*.

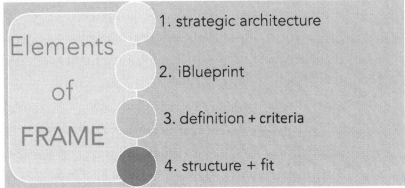

Figure 2. The four elements of FRAME.

1. Strategic architecture

I once hosted an innovation workshop for the top twenty-five senior executives of a large multinational manufacturing company. I gave the following assignment as prework:

- Working in pairs, go on a strategic architecture scavenger hunt.
- Using the punch list provided, find a document and file for each item.
- Bring these to the first day of the workshop.
- If you can't find a document or file, find the person who might be able to describe it and bring the results of that description to the workshop.

The executives had more than two months to complete the assignment. The right-hand column in Table 1 shows the results of what one pair of executives found in their scavenger hunt.

Strategic Architecture Scavenger Hunt Results	
Punch List	*Findings*
Enterprise Description	Found in the board chair's slide deck for onboarding new board members
Aspirations of the Company	Found in CEO's presentation in the annual shareholders' meeting, as recorded in the transcript.
Enterprise Strategy	Compiled from presentation slides for the annual senior leadership meeting and the 10-year product plans found in each business unit.
Vision and Mission	Vision and mission were not separated, but we found marketing materials describing it. Not sure if it is enterprise-wide or for that business unit.
Values	Values found on the company website under the tab "Join our Company."
Direction for the Businesses	Found in presentation slides from quarterly operations reviews. Could roll up annual performance plans, but did not have time, access, or resources.
Overview of the Strategic Architecture	Not found, assume it exists in CEO's head. Thought about setting up a meeting with her, decided not to.

Table 1.

When we saw similarly lackluster results from the other pairs, we discussed what the executives could do to remedy the situation and how that remedy would improve their innovation effort. Again, this is not a poorly run company. In my experience, these results are typical for most companies. The bottom line? Organizations have a ways to go to perfect what I call their *strategic architecture* for innovation.

Strategic architecture is the alignment of the enterprise vision, mission, strategies, goals, and values. Although it can take many forms, practically speaking it represents a set of decisions that leaders in your company should make to help execute your strategy.

In a general sense, *strategic architecture*:

- Is a formal description of the enterprise
- Is future-oriented
- Includes enterprise strategy with a summary of top-line goals, areas of focus, competitive advantage, markets, businesses, and assets
- Includes mission, vision, and values
- Sets direction for businesses and for every employee
- Shows how elements of the strategic architecture are connected
- Is found in one place and is easy to read and understand

One of the best approaches for making *strategic architecture* succinct can be found in Robert S. Kaplan and David P. Norton's work on strategy maps.[8] A strategy map is a simple, concise rendering of your *strategic architecture*. You can adapt the strategy map template to fit your company. The approach seems deceptively simple, but the real work occurs behind the scenes as you struggle to align perspectives and characterize your *strategic architecture* on a single sheet. If your company has a strategy map, every innovation team can begin there and use it to guide them through the evolution of their innovation process.

The Innovation Universe positions *strategic architecture* as an element in FRAME. It necessitates organizational alignment around a series of decisions. The decisions specific to a strategy map include, but are not limited to, these questions:

- Do we already have something like this?
- If not, do we need a strategy map?
- If we choose to create one, do we create one or several?
- If we have several, how are they aligned?
- How do we communicate strategy maps?

Creating a strategy map may not be in your job description. Regardless, your innovation teams will need it to align their efforts and work toward executing the organization's overall strategy. If you take it upon yourself to help initiate the strategy map, use caution to avoid triggering your company's immune system. Understandably, companies are proprietary about their strategy and sensitive about the format documentation takes. Exercise good judgment about how to start the process: include the right people within the company and understand who has approval rights. Regardless of how it comes to life, a document that describes your company's *strategic architecture* for every member of your innovation teams, and every employee for that matter, is essential to the short- and long-term success of innovation.

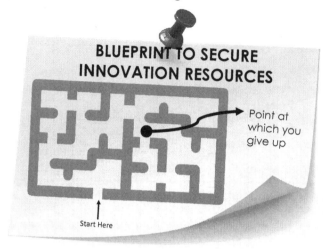

Innovation Pivot 6.

2. iBlueprint

When I started as the head of innovation for Whirlpool, one of the first things the executive committee asked me to do was create an innovation strategy, or blueprint. I was lost. I searched for a sample but came up empty. (In the early days of innovation, it was hard to find best practices.) Looking back, I am embarrassed at how rudimentary my *iBlueprint* was, but it served its purpose. The executive committee gave me the following guidelines:

- Create a three-year plan for innovation aligned with the business strategy
- Focus on the core business
- Unleash innovation that adds value to the company through bottom-line, organic growth

- Facilitate senior leader alignment
- Ensure customer-centered innovation
- Build innovation as a core competency
- Seek innovation from everyone and everywhere
- Embed innovation into every job

Simply stated, an *iBlueprint* is your strategic plan for an innovation initiative, and it should align with the business strategy. After seeing blueprints from many different companies over the years, I assembled this assortment of items to incorporate as you put yours together:

- The problem you are trying to solve
- Innovation definition
- Communications to all employees
- Types of innovations
- Tools and approaches
- Measuring, tracking, and reporting
- Resource utilization
- Governance and role definitions
- Training requirements
- Recognition and rewards

Creating an *iBlueprint* forces you think critically about innovation planning and strategy. One effective way to create such a blueprint and to differentiate it from business strategy is to employ a simple five-page outline.

iBlueprint Outline	
Page 1: **WHY**	Title of blueprint Add your strategy map here
Page 2: **WHAT**	Problem you are trying to solve, scope and benefits from innovation, with emphasis on customer benefits; innovation *definition*; what you intend to learn (or what you don't know); horizons, markets, and customers that innovation will target.
Page 3: **HOW**	Types and approaches; what has worked to date; measurements, resources (time, people, money), training, communications, and recognition.
Page 4: **WHO**	Role definitions, including the parts of the company that will be involved, leadership accountabilities, governance, and alignment within the company (key people, other initiatives, business planning cycle considerations).
Page 5: **WHEN**	Next steps, timing, milestones, immediate problems to address, how you will show quick (less than six months) results.

Table 2.

Crafting an *iBlueprint* is an essential exercise because it not only creates a strategy document, but also starts a dialogue within your company that creates alignment and removes the barriers to success. Two areas to consider as you are creating your *iBlueprint* are horizons and types of innovations.

Horizons describe the maturity and relative risk of future growth opportunities. They allow companies to manage a portfolio of projects for current and future growth.[9] There are multiple articles and frameworks on business horizons and the role innovation can play in each. McKinsey's classic *Three Horizons of Growth* presents perhaps the most authoritative perspective on the topic.[10] This model uses a trio of concurrent horizons to help you keep your business focused on growth and innovation:

- Horizon 1: Maintain and Defend the Core Business
- Horizon 2: Nurture Emerging Businesses
- Horizon 3: Create New Businesses

I use this model with senior innovation teams to help them create their *iBlueprints*. It is particularly relevant in the early stages of innovation planning as you put a stake in the ground. For example, you can begin to innovate at the core of the business and migrate outward to other horizons once you develop a set of innovation skills. Likewise, the model can help you think about innovation from a portfolio perspective across all three horizons.

Types

A second main element to consider as part of your *iBlueprint* is what types of innovations your company wants to pursue. To get started in your inquiry, take a look at the groundbreaking work from Deloitte and Doblin, led by Larry Keeley, entitled "Ten Types of Innovation."[11] Your company may want to start with one or two types, gain a set of skills, and then move to try others. The Doblin ten types, nested in three elements, are:

- **Configuration:** Profit Model, Network, Structure, and Process
- **Offering:** Product Performance and Product System
- **Experience:** Service, Channel, Brand, and Customer Engagement

While you can decide on a case-by-case basis whether to include any or all of these in your *iBlueprint*, I want to draw your attention to the next FRAME element that deserves a closer look: *definition + criteria*.

3. Definition + criteria

A services company came to me to help them stem the downward spiral occurring in their innovation effort. Using the Innovation Universe framework, it became clear to me that the firm had bypassed a critical element in the process: deciding how it would define innovation.

It is essential to include a working definition of (or set of criteria for) innovation as part of your *iBlueprint*, in part to determine how much of your revenue will come from innovative products or services. For most companies, that percentage will not be 100 percent, especially if the bar for what passes for innovation is set sufficiently high. You will also use the *definition* to track innovations in the marketplace and report progress. In general, a *definition* is critical for aligning expectations and measuring the success of an innovation initiative.

The innovation *definition* should include a description of the unique qualities required for a product/service to be considered "innovative" by your company and customers. As part of that, a *definition* can serve as a filter and prioritization mechanism. For instance, you can use it to triage offerings that are less relevant to your strategy and rank the remaining offerings as they relate to customer needs. In addition, any *definition* or *criteria* should include what you hope to achieve through innovation. For example, for a product or service to be considered innovative at Whirlpool, it has to meet all three of these criteria:

- Unique and compelling to our customer
- Creates sustainable competitive advantage
- Creates superior shareholder value

Although unassuming, it took a lot more work and alignment than you might think to get to this *definition*. Because of its specificity, the *definition* became the lingua franca at Whirlpool for defining innovation, thereby setting up an opportunity to treat innovation as a core business process. Table 3 shows some additional definitions for different industries:

Innovation Definition Examples

Pharma	• A unique product or service that improves a patient's life. • Furthers the business strategy. • Creates a positive and sustainable ROI.
State Government	• Substantially improves efficiency in existing processes and procedures. • Creates significant savings in either employee time or budgetary cost. • Creates new services of material value to citizens without increasing the total bottom line of the state/agency budget.
Services	• Provides services that are unique, risk-aware, and reliable. • Helps create new markets or extends reach from the core. • Increases efficiency of operations by cutting costs, not head count.
Insurance	• Encourages development of new products or services that create value and leverage our capabilities. • Addresses the needs of our target consumer segments in unique, differentiated, and sustainable ways.
Consumer Products	• A new or improved product, process, or service that creates value. • Is the result of addressing existing problems and unmet needs.
Business to Business	• Any idea that changes something to better serve your customer. • Can be anything from a process to a product to an internal system, with a focus on efficiency and quality.

Table 3.

Keep in mind that if you are going to create a *definition*, it should set a very high bar. I worked with one company where only 15 percent of their total offerings qualified as innovation. All the rest of their products were equally important; they were simply not considered innovative.

In my workshops and consulting, defining innovation creates lively discussions. In fact, about one-third of the companies I work with decide not to develop a *definition* at all. One company abstained because it felt that everything the firm created should be innovative. Another company did not want to categorize products as innovative—it felt this would confuse employees. Still other companies believe that defining innovation will limit success or focus too much senior leadership attention on how much value innovation is creating. It's your choice to make.

Innovation Pivot 6.

4. Structure +fit

Structure + fit help position innovation within your organization and align it with other strategic priorities. *Structure* refers to how you will organize your innovation effort.

There are countless ways to think about *structure*. An excellent first step is to look at how your company structures other successful strategic initiatives. For example, if you have Six Sigma black belts in each unit, you may want to replicate that with *iMentors* (facilitators of innovation) in each unit. If you plan to innovate with partner companies or start-ups, you may decide to structure the initiative in a fashion similar to your other partner-driven strategic initiatives. A few key questions pertaining to *structure*:

- Will you have an overall lead, distributed leads, or no lead?
- To whom will the innovation lead report?
- How will you resource the effort?
- Will there be a governance body to oversee innovation?

Fit addresses how innovation will harmonize with other key initiatives in your strategy. I recently conducted a custom workshop for a large manufacturing company where all of the stars seemed to be aligned to launch an innovation effort at record speed. Then they hit a speed bump. As they worked through the Innovation Universe framework, they experienced a setback when it came to *fit*. It turned out that their other key initiative was a multiyear Six Sigma program that was widely considered to be the backbone of the company. When they introduced innovation, it was unclear to everyone how it would *fit* with the Six Sigma effort.

To address this issue, it is vital for architects of innovation to understand how new projects will complement other key initiatives. Leaders need to not only envision the synergy but also communicate it across the company. Otherwise, employees will be confused, and innovation will fail to achieve its full potential. It is better to create the connections on the front end, even knowing that genuine synergy grows and changes over time. As a rule of thumb, planning in advance is preferable to letting confusion create a black cloud over innovation.

FRAME *takeaways*

The FRAME foundation in the Innovation Universe is a valuable leadership tool. It starts a necessary dialogue and defines a set of decisions that create a robust backstory to help innovation thrive. Without FRAME, innovation and innovators are left without a North Star, traveling through darkness without the coordinates to reach their destination. These are the top things to keep in mind about FRAME:

- You need a clear, consistent strategy that is defined and searchable, everyone can get their hands on it and it is common knowledge across the company.

- FRAME guides you to harmonize innovation with other key initiatives in your company. For example, it helps you understand and articulate up front how innovation and operational excellence are codependent.

- FRAME spells out how innovation will benefit the company, with an emphasis on adding value for customers.

- If your company has inadequate framing for innovation, it is up to you to remedy this by making the appropriate framing decisions within your leadership domain. Even if FRAME is not an explicit part of your job description, stepping up and taking responsibility can mean the difference between success and failure in getting the resources and support for innovation.

CHAPTER 3

GENERATE
Customer-driven
problem solving

The way I see it, you have three choices in life: consume,
critique, or create. I prefer the latter.

I n front of you is a large, main-se-
quenced star located in the spiral arm
of the Universe, orbited by all of the
foundations, supplying the heat and
light that sustain growth. Welcome to
the sun of the Innovation Universe.

GENERATE's focus is discovering and implementing customer-driven problem solving. GENERATE is about moving
from concept to commercialization, and it includes innovations of all types and in all areas of growth, in both existing
and new markets. It includes incremental as well as breakthrough innovations. GENERATE is the innovation foundation that conferences, workshops, books, and companies focus on the most, and it is where organizations put the majority of their resources and effort.

In the early days of innovation at Whirlpool Corporation,
Inspired Chef™ was considered to be an exciting new business model. According to the trademark filed in 2000,[12] Inspired Chef (IC) consisted of "retail store services, via in-store
sale, in-home direct sale, mail order, and internet catalog

sale, featuring kitchen utensils, specialty food ingredients, and small appliances." On a practical level, part of IC included contracting with chefs to bring state-of-the-art cooking tools and appliances for sale during cooking classes and dinner parties. At the time, it was an innovative way for Whirlpool to meet customers in new retail spaces and include them in the innovation process. From a strategic perspective, IC was a concept designed to help the company move beyond selling appliances to creating customer experiences. It helped the company forge new business models around branded cooking appliances offered by Whirlpool. Ultimately, it became an innovation extension of the KitchenAid brand.[13]

In the initial stages of the project, the IC team researched cooking trends, family routines, competitive offerings, market discontinuities, and technologies that might uncover new and relevant cooking products and experiences. They analyzed orthodoxies and core competencies related to the IC space. Once the IC team finished their discovery phase, they began to ideate variations on cooking products and experiences that would delight customers. As this period coincided with the dawn of celebrity chefs, they also forged partnerships with cooking icons and other industry brands.

The IC team built several prototypes (products and experiences) and invited input from customers, both at-home cooks and professional chefs. They used what they learned to develop and refine products and services. All the while, they were vetting the innovation within the company to gain internal alignment and support. The IC team launched the innovations about six months after their initial ideation phase. They continued to adapt and improve the lineup post-launch.

Inspired Chef had a great run. It was in the marketplace for several years until the company ultimately discontinued it, or as Whirlpool would say, "shelved" it.

Yet, I would argue that great innovations can't really be shelved. Instead, they go underground and resurface in various forms and iterations as opportunities arise. Looking back, the various IC solutions and ideas lived on in the company's institutional memory long after IC was discontinued. The solutions and ideas resurfaced in stories, as artifacts, and with the employees—many of whom continued their work for the company and developed other innovations, perhaps with the subliminal IC experience as a touchstone. The IC team and their work hatched several associated innovations, directly or indirectly, for years to come.

Ultimately, Whirlpool's business morphed and migrated in radical new ways. For over a century, the business model was to build and sell products, in consultation with retailers, through a B2B model. IC helped the company move into online retail and create a cadence of cooking accessories and customer experiences and relationships. Whirlpool opened branded retail spaces in several countries worldwide and opened an "experience and training center" in Chicago for commercial partners. IC alone did not create these successive innovations and I doubt everyone at Whirlpool would agree entirely with my view of the migration of this particular innovation. But most would concur that IC altered our idea of what an appliance brand could be. It paved the way for expansive thinking and actions around cooking products and experiences. It did what great innovations should do: It broke new ground both in the marketplace and in the company that created it.

Collateral successes

In my innovation workshops, practitioners often get into a spirited debate about "failure" and how to use that term. Our discussion of failure inevitably percolates around questions such as:

- Is meeting launch goals the key indicator of success or failure?
- Do innovations need to be new to the world and last forever to be viewed as successful?
- Can incremental innovation be considered a success, or does every innovation need to disrupt?

Interpreting the results of innovation is not a universal science; there are gray areas. Often, we are quick to judge innovations based on financials and customer feedback, and for good reason. However, maintaining a long-term perspective on the collateral successes that innovations yield can shed new light on results. After all, every attempt at innovation can bring a company one step closer to its next great success in the marketplace. Innovation outcomes can also draw a firm closer to the insight and learning that ultimately creates a culture of innovation that pays a myriad of dividends for an organization and its employees.

In fact, the word "inspired" in the Inspired Chef program did not apply just to the set of innovations it delivered to customers. It was also inspiring to observe the innovators at work and play. Their passion, hard work, and professionalism was contagious. They moved through the innovation process and initiated the organizational changes required for success. Although Inspired Chef was one of many innovations coming from Whirlpool during that period, I chose to describe IC because it demonstrates the GENERATE foundation in the Innovation Universe, not through charts, text, or graphs but with a story of success and failure, facts and emotions, and innovation heroes who inspire me to this day. IC forever changed Whirlpool's DNA and moved the organization one step closer to innovation from *everyone and everywhere.*

What is your Inspired Chef?

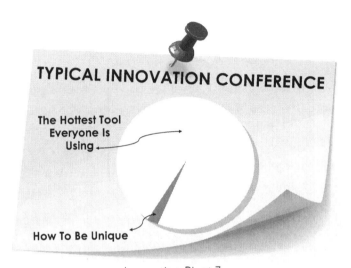

Innovation Pivot 7.

Putting GENERATE into context

Chances are your company has some experience generating innovations. But if you want to position innovation as a core business process, you have to understand the fundamental tenets that underlie the GENERATE foundation.

First, the GENERATE foundation should create a cadence of innovations. The goal is not to be one-and-done but to create successive innovations. That means moving beyond innovation as a unique event to creating a common-cause mindset where innovation is "always on." Next, GENERATE ensures that innovation is customer-centered. For many companies, becoming customer-centered is the most difficult part of their innovation transformation. Finally, GENERATE is a problem-solving methodology that uses both adaptive and technical applications to reach its goal.

Yet, to fully embrace these and other benefits of the GENERATE foundation, companies need to bypass the barriers to innovation that are so common in an organizational setting. For instance, there is a pervasive belief among innovators that the processes that make organizations sustainable are hostile to innovation efforts. Conventional wisdom says that innovation needs to be spontaneous and unbounded to achieve creativity, and that bureaucratic processes derail innovation. That's arguably true. However, within this idea lies an orthodoxy that we can work to overturn, not only to preserve spontaneity and creativity, but also to allow innovation to thrive in the context of companies and teams.

To do that, we need to rethink some of the basics of how we view processes in companies. For example, let's agree that innovation is rarely the result of lone-wolf actors. Rather, innovation in companies is the result of diverse and successive teams that create insights and systematically turn them into commercial innovations. Many employees will touch that innovation as it heads to market. In addition, innovation must be purposefully embedded in all aspects of your company to make it work in the long term. This means innovation can't be isolated as a "skunkworks." Instead, every role in the company should be viewed as an innovation role, just as every role in consumer product companies is focused in some way on quality or safety. In other words, successful innovation requires process.

With this in mind, we can build processes that support innovation instead of rules that hinder it. After all, innovation that occurs across boundaries such as companies, time zones, functions, investors, language, technologies, cultures, and networks require a common process and language to make it feasible.

Yes, I will grant you that process can travel on a continuum from very good (on the right of the continuum) to very bad (on the left). Many companies have a hard time staying on the right side of process even as they venture to innovate. They often add more and more structure and requirements as time goes on: more forms, more compliance, and more steps, until they lose sight of the innovation itself. But for the purposes of exploring GENERATE in the Innovation Universe, let's position process on the good side of the continuum. In the spirit of learning, let's neutralize it by viewing it as something that is inherently neither positive nor negative—understanding that, left to our own devices, we all have a left-leaning tendency on the process continuum. If we think about process as a way to deliver innovation—as opposed to a means for constraining it—it takes some of the sting out of the processes we need to run companies.

We will address organizational change and processes further below and again in EMBED and LEAD. For now, let's set it aside and take a closer look at the elements of GENERATE as a means for customer-driven problem solving.

If FRAME is the North Star in the Innovation Universe, then GENERATE is the sun. The other three foundations, FRAME, EMBED, and LEAD, rotate around GENERATE. In fact, they are in service to GENERATE. Often the term "innovation" is used as a proxy for GENERATE, but in the Innovation, Universe GENERATE is:

> The process and methods used to develop innovations, from insights to commercialization, that are valued by the customer. Bringing a cadence of innovations to market that help create competitive advantage.

GENERATE is the engine that creates innovations in the marketplace. It is:

- The capability to deliver unique solutions (product and nonproduct) that create value for customers and companies.
- Best typified as an innovation project or a series of innovation projects that help organizations grow and expand into existing or new markets.
- What companies track and measure to understand their success in innovation.

The Four Elements of GENERATE

The four elements of GENERATE offer a set of decisions about how you create and deliver innovations. These elements range from the approach you might use and the structure for teams, to reaching out to partners, and to monitoring progress of your company's innovations.

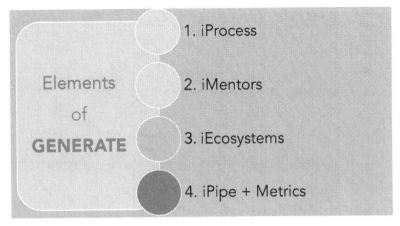

Figure 3. The four elements of GENERATE.

1. iProcess

One of the essential decisions you will make in the GEN-ERATE foundation is to select your unifying process for in-novation, which I call an *iProcess*. In general, having an *iProcess* enables you to track the progress of innovation within your company. It also codifies a common language and set of tools to be shared and passed down as new innovation teams form. In general, an *iProcess* creates an efficient path for innovation and knowledge sharing that levels the playing field for all current and future innovators in the company.

To be sure, there is no shortage of turnkey *iProcesses*. Well-known "branded" methodologies today include Lean Start-Up, Design Thinking, Empathetic Design, Lenses, and Reverse Innovation, as well as many others that are named after the consulting firms, universities, or academics who created them. These are all viable, and oftentimes desirable and feasible, depending on your company's needs.

For all but the most entrenched innovation professionals,

sorting out which branded *iProcess* to use can be difficult because they change so frequently. Some processes get more oxygen than others, regardless of quality, and it is not always clear how they differ. Blending them to get the most from each is intimidating at best.

For our purposes, the Innovation Universe is brand-agnostic and does not recommend any one *iProcess*. Instead, it uses the Unifying Innovation Methodology (UIM) that is based on common traits and steps from many branded *iProcesses*. Ideally, the UIM will give you the basic knowledge you need to select a branded *iProcess* or blend the ideas to create your own.

The UIM was formulated in 2012 when a small group of innovation practitioners, including myself, met to create a leading-edge curriculum at the University of Notre Dame to train innovation leaders and practitioners. We quickly faced the problem of what branded *iProcess* to use.

Our experience was that almost all *iProcesses* are trying to do the same thing—create a path for innovation. Yet, they each have specific nuances and different terms that make them difficult to compare. The UIM uses general terms for each step and offers a holistic view of an *iProcess*. It is tailored for the corporate setting and it begins one step before most of the branded *iProcesses*. After the Target pre-step, the innovation phases of the UIM are Discover, Ideate, Elaborate, and Launch.

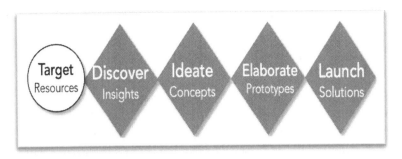

Figure 4. The Unifying Innovation Methodology.[14]

Although the UIM appears orderly in the Figure 4, in practice it is iterative and messy. Don't think of the UIM as an arrow shot from one end of the process to the other. Instead, it is a series of actions akin to a jumbled set of arrows that go in many different directions, looping back on themselves as you move from Target to Launch.

Target resources: Secure support

Target is the UIM pre-step where successful innovation teams in companies align their thinking with leaders about strategy, customers, potential new products, and service concepts. This critical pre-step is a best estimate at the beginning of the innovation process that innovators refine and revise as they progress toward Launch. The Target pre-step includes a strategy map or linkages, a rough concept of the innovation, potential customers, a discussion of competitors, general business model assumptions and financials, description of the innovation team, and an estimate of resources required to get the innovation through the first phase or tollgate. Target becomes a charter, a living document that changes as the innovation team progresses through the innovation phases. This is also where innovators stretch their thinking and describe their innovation dream state.

This pre-step is a scoping and planning mechanism to not only align the innovation team with the decision makers in the company, but also to align the members of the team with each other. As new members of the team or new entities in the *iEcosystem* join, the Target charter becomes an onboarding vehicle. By the time the team reaches the Elaborate phase, where they will have detailed financials, they can replace the Target charter with a business plan for the innovation. The bottom line is that the Target pre-step saves time and allows innovation teams to move faster. Most of the established branded innovation processes don't start with Target, yet I would argue that it is a vital first step for innovating within a company.

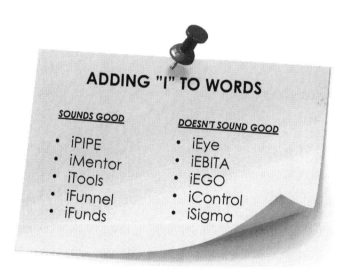

ADDING "I" TO WORDS

SOUNDS GOOD	DOESN'T SOUND GOOD
• iPIPE	• iEye
• iMentor	• iEBITA
• iTools	• iEGO
• iFunnel	• iControl
• iFunds	• iSigma

Innovation Pivot 8.

Discover is the first innovation phase of the UIM. Its goal is to disrupt established mental frames and encourage you to look at your potential innovation in a bigger space. If you are asked to design the next stand mixer, for instance, most innovation teams will jump in with ideas to add new attachments, make it cord-free, or redesign the bowl to expand functionality. All great ideas, right?

Discover says,

Not so fast, we will get there, but first let's learn more about the space around the mixer.

Using a set of tools or lenses, Discover guides innovators to research trends such as eating habits, family traits, kitchen design, and food preparation. It starts with collecting insights from present and potential customers. It also guides innovators to look at external canvasses such as competitors, technology, and trends. Tools you might use here include a technology map, orthodoxies, competitor analysis, customer empathy, and analogs. Regardless of the specifics, all of the tools in this phase are intended to expand your thinking.

Discover is a divergent phase. It allows for expansive thinking before innovation teams create ideas and offer solutions. In our stand mixer example, the desired output would be to discover and catalog hundreds or thousands of insights. Innovators write each insight on a sticky note with a reference number for a source that, if used later in the process, can be traced. The beauty of using sticky notes is that they are very low-tech, mobile, and tactile.

Discover gives innovation teams a deeper, more empathetic, and intellectual connection to the problem they are trying to solve. It forces innovators to slow down and understand the problem; it keeps them from jumping to any one solution or conclusion too fast. Discover also helps create a competitive advantage. Any innovation team can come up with the idea to make the stand mixer cordless; it is the profound new insights at the intersections of ideas that contribute to new-to-the world innovations.

Yes, Discover adds time to the process. In a time-starved world, many innovation teams choose to skip Discover and start with Ideate. Sometimes this is necessary and even appropriate. I have found that for products or services in business units, Discover can be accomplished once every two or three years—using the interim time to harvest the many ideas that come out of that stage.

If you skip Discover, you have some decisions to make. For example, if a consultant introduces an innovation ideation process in your company, be sure you understand how the innovators will break frames before they create ideas. Find out how they will come to profoundly appreciate the customer and the space around the proposed innovation. Decide if more time and effort is needed to research and understand the bigger picture. If your objective is a new-to-the-world product or service, it is essential for you to figure out how your innovation teams will break frames in Discover.

CARRY WITH YOU AT **ALL** TIMES

Innovation

Failed, but
Learned a Ton!

THIS CARD MAY BE KEPT UNTIL NEEDED OR SOLD
Get Out of *(TALENT POOL)* **JAIL FREE**

Innovation Pivot 9.

Ideate: Conceive new solutions

Ideate takes all of the findings gathered in Discover, as well as native knowledge and insights from the innovation team, and merges these findings into bundles of ideas that become preliminary innovation concepts.

One way to do this is through an idea lab (iLab). Imagine a studio space with all of the sticky notes from the Discover insights. They are spread out on tables and panels. You and a partner start to pair disparate insights into bundled concepts. Through a facilitated *iProcess*, you can look for intersections and begin to discover and describe something new to the world.

Ideate does something else that is critical within a company: it gives "permission to innovate." It is astonishing how many people have ideas or the predispositions to create new concepts, but they sit back, waiting to be invited. Ideate not only asks for ideas but also provides potential innovators with a safe space to try them out. Ideate equips innovators with tools to bring new ideas to the world. Where Discover holds innovators back from coming up with solutions prematurely, Ideate unleashes them. Most branded *iProcesses* excel at Ideate, so almost any will be a safe selection in this phase of your *iProcess*. Your decisions in Ideate will include:

- Which branded iProcess to use
- How to render and organize the ideas
- How to prioritize the ideas into a few concepts that will go to the next phase

In Ideate, innovators diverge to look for new ideas and then converge on a few concepts that customers will value.

Elaborate: Create viable offerings

In the Elaborate phase, the goal is to create, test, and prepare products or services to go to market. You will run experiments and create prototypes as you get closer and closer to a final offering. You will refine the business model and go-to-market plans that will help you navigate the Launch process. Often in Elaborate, if not before, companies may have "tollgates," which are the part of the approval process. Senior leaders or stakeholders will weigh in on the innovation to determine the go/no-go decision before your company invests significant time and resources in scaling the innovation for Launch.

Elaborate ends the expansive development journey as the *iProcess* moves into tangible and refined products and services with goals, *metrics*, and go-to-market plans. In a product company, a product development process may merge with the *iProcess* here to take the product to market. Elaborate begins the de-risking portion of the UIM.

Launch: Extract value

The last phase in the UIM is Launch. Launch is where you commercialize innovations and, ideally, extract value. It also includes post-Launch tracking and using innovation and marketing/sales tools to extend the product's or service's life cycle. Surprisingly, many branded *iProcesses* omit this phase.

I worked with one company that launched innovations, patted themselves on the back, and went straight to the next one without tracking or managing the last innovation post-Launch. Sound crazy? It's common in some companies. In this case, the company eventually recognized the problem. As they told me, "We realized that we do not so much as launch products, as let them escape." After that, they set a goal to move from "Launch & Leave" to "Launch & Love."

iProcess and UIM Summary

The UIM is a generalized *iProcess* within the GENERATE foundation. From Target to Launch, it clarifies and simplifies the common innovation steps from branded *iProcesses* and slows down the action long enough for you to understand the universal steps and proposed outcomes. At every phase in the *iProcess*, companies have decisions to make that are specific to their unique circumstances. Once you master the UIM, you can look at any branded *iProcess* and understand how it might perform in your company. You can also look at an *iProcess* and analyze where it might underperform. Understanding the UIM can help you conduct targeted benchmarking to get the "nugget" you need to move your company's *iProcess* to the next level. Finally, when you have the right *iProcess* for your company, innovation can be taught and learned as part of the quest to spark innovation from everyone and everywhere.

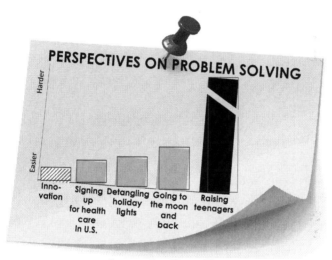

Innovation Pivot 10.

2. iMentors

The second element in the GENERATE foundation is *iMentors*. *iMentors* are loosely equivalent to master black belts in Six Sigma. They are the highly trained facilitators of your innovation process who help teams get from Target through Launch. They are not the innovators, per se, but *iMentors* help enable innovations within your company. In fact, *iMentors* are often the employees' first stop when they have an idea. *iMentors* will help them take the idea to the next level, locate like-minded stakeholders, or connect them with innovators who are working on compatible projects. In addition, *iMentors* often pitch in on some innovation tasks, like competitive research or due diligence, while the business group is putting out fires or otherwise occupied.

iMentors can be part-time or full-time roles assigned to reside within a business unit or float among several departments. Sometimes *iMentors* rotate between several organizations. In fact, I know networks of companies that use a common *iProcess* and exchange *iMentors*, sharing resources to keep up with their peaks and mitigate their valleys during innovation cycles.

In some cases, *iMentors* volunteer for the role and in others they are selected or appointed by leaders or the appropriate internal talent-pool committee. Regardless of the selection specifics, *iMentors* need to know your *iProcess* and be trained in innovation, group dynamics, coaching, storytelling, and facilitation skills. *iMentors* teach and share new information and delight in helping teams experience the "aha" moment of innovation. In fact, they are often drawn or recruited to the role because they are lifelong learners who value new knowledge.

I have helped to train thousands of *iMentors*. I also teach in the University of Notre Dame Executive Education innovation curricula for *iMentors*, where we offer open enrollment and custom workshops for companies. Although *iMentors* are all different, the training process has some commonalities. After learning the steps of innovation, *iMentors* practice their craft by facilitating a number of different innovation projects to gain exposure to different business models. There is also typically a certification process that includes a peer review of their body of work and a sample project. The process usually includes testing as well, plus a requirement to write an innovation post or article that demonstrates their thought leadership in innovation.

If a company has more than a few *iMentors*, they generally meet as a network to exchange ideas and share new innovation tools or models. Individually or as a network, *iMentors* see patterns across the innovation projects to which they are assigned. Thus, they can be excellent as a resource for leaders who need to learn how an innovation initiative is progressing on the front lines. *iMentors* can also act as a sounding board and help you implement solutions to advance innovation in any setting within your company.

Whether to have *iMentors* and how to formulate an *iMentor* program entails an additional set of decisions that the Innovation Universe can help you navigate. Depending on what you decide and how you structure your program, the advantages of *iMentors* include:

- Trained experts to help innovators
- Instant assistance for employees who have an innovation idea
- Competitive advantage with strategic partners who need innovation help
- Detailed insight and feedback on your innovation initiative
- A career track that attracts talent to your company
- Leaner innovation projects due to experienced facilitation

But there might be disadvantages:

- An iMentor program may be perceived as an added cost.
- iMentors are candidates to be cut first during cost reduction.
- If part-time, prioritizing iMentors' time for innovation projects is a challenge.
- Accountability for the iMentor program must be assigned and resourced.
- There may be confusion about iMentors' role in the company and/or innovation process.

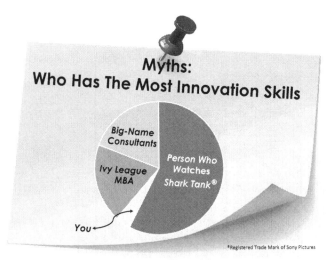

Innovation Pivot 11.

When the goal within a company is to GENERATE innovation from everyone and everywhere, training employees solely in a static classroom setting is not a proper approach. Using *iMentors*, workshops, proto-types, just-in-time training, and facilitation can offer advantages for getting a broad audience of employees trained in innovation. If *iMentors* in particular are not the right answer for you, you can decide on another path for training and mentoring innovators to ensure that projects move along on target and that innovation is embedded as a core competency in every role in your company.

3. iEcosystems

iEcosystems, the next element in GENERATE, centers on collaboration. iEcosystems involve collaboration with partners, employees, and innovators required to move innovations from idea to commercialization.

This element entails forging partnerships with labs, innovation scouts, compatible organizations, and investors, as well as other innovators inside and outside of your company. Why bother with *iEcosystems*? The upside is enormous: partnerships and other facets of *iEcosystems* can make innovation efforts far more fruitful by virtue of the exchange of expertise and ideas as well as the efficiencies of scale that collaborations afford.

To make the most of *iEcosystems*, innovators need to have access to certain basic tools that make partnering possible, including an Intellectual Property (IP) strategy, funding models, nondisclosure agreements (NDAs), ownership guidelines, a clear path for approval, and legal and talent considerations, to name a few. If you are the innovation initiative lead, then think through the minimal support you need in place before you can unleash innovators into the world in search of partners and collaborators.

Your minimal support should not only help innovators, but also protect your company. In other words, clear guidelines and guardrails need to be put in place to govern everything from the ownership of ideas to future payouts. Innovators need to understand the parameters before they enter into partnerships.

Other decision points in the *iEcosystems* element include the full partnership process and *metrics* for deciding what deals and deal structures are most appropriate.

- Will you use your unifying iProcess (and perhaps your *iMentors*) in your work with partners?
- How will you measure the value-add and ROI of each partnership?
- How will you share partnership lessons learned across innovation teams?
- How will you communicate partnerships within the organization and to outside stakeholders?

For some companies, simply identifying appropriate innovation partners and forming an *iEcosystem* can be a significant hurdle. In most cases, I suggest starting with your installed base. Existing strategic partners, from vendors and distributors to commercial partners, are excellent candidates. Your company partner-relationship leads can also identify entities that share your interests and passion for innovation exploration. Or you can use innovation scouts to help reach out to technology companies, universities, labs, consortiums, start-ups, and incubators. One thing that large organizations have to offer potential partners is scale. In many cases, start-ups and other early-stage companies can benefit from your established distribution channels, technology, and customer segments.

Beyond being proactive, it also pays to put your company out there so that partners can find you. Decide on ways to communicate your sandbox through conferences, articles, blogs, podcasts, and industry associations. Look at your website to see if there is a section that invites collaboration.

The final element to consider in order to form and fully leverage *iEcosystems* is your company's reputation. Word gets around fast if your leadership team is hard to work with, your organization is burdened by bureaucracy, or your dealmakers are heavy-handed in ownership positions. Keep an eye on your reputation and work hard at being a preferred partner.

4. iPipe + metrics

The last element in GENERATE is the Innovation Pipeline (*iPipe*) and *metrics*. This element involves tracking and measuring products/services that meet the definition/criteria of innovation. The *iPipe* is a visual representation of the innovations that are progressing through the *iProcess* toward Launch. The steps in the pipeline generally match the phases in your *iProcess*. For example, if we use the UIM, an associated *iPipe* may be as simple as the one depicted in Figure 5.

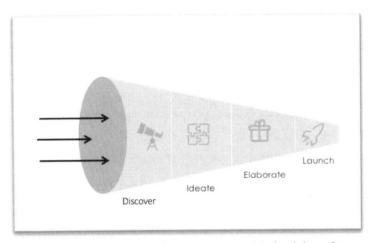

Figure 5. iPipe using the Unifying Innovation Methodology Stages.

In product companies, stage-gate is a standard process for monitoring and managing new product development. If you use stage-gate or another established development process, you can help your company decide how to combine or merge it with your *iProcess*. Often companies will put the *iProcess* at the fuzzy front end of development and harmonize the intermediate steps to fit both innovation and product development needs.

The visual representation of the innovation as depicted through *iPipe* should include the appropriate *metrics*. You can create *metrics* that help you understand factors such as speed, breakage, risk factors, and estimated versus actual value created, among others. Depending on where your specific innovation initiative is struggling, you can add measures that help you overcome challenges. For example, if you find that it takes five hundred ideas in the fuzzy front end of your *iPipe* to launch one innovation, you can determine how to optimize the number of ideas needed in the pipeline to fulfill your innovation goals. Another way to use the *iPipe* is to analyze failure modes. For example, you might find that a majority of innovations fail in the Elaborate phase. With that, you and your *iMentors* can analyze the activities in Elaborate and make changes in the tools, leadership sponsors, and partners to help more innovations make it through the process.

The *metrics* you select for GENERATE are relative to where your company is in its innovation initiative. If you are just getting started, your *metrics* might be more *input* in nature. If you have launched innovations into the marketplace, you may have *output metrics*. The following chart outlines the most common *metrics* found in innovation programs:

Examples of Innovation Metrics

Input	Process	Output
• Number of people trained • Number of ideas generated • Innovation expenses (time, funds, FTEs, capital) • Employee awareness • Internal management systems realigned • Number of trained iMentors	• iPipe analytics • Number/efficacy of external collaborators • Targets or milestones achieved • Compensation and performance appraisals based on innovation activities	• New iRevenue • ROI on innovation spend • Market share metrics • Customer metrics • Product/service metrics • Quality, cost, safety • Payback period • Cannibalization of existing offerings • New patents, media hits, brand strength, iEcosystems

Table 4.[15]

The decisions in *iPipe + metrics* include:

- Whether or not to create an iPipe
- What form it will take
- What measures to use
- How to communicate results, including bottom-line financials

If you aim to EMBED innovation as a core business process, along with *iPipe + metrics*, it is essential that the innovation *metrics* be on par with the metrics of other key business processes in your company.

GENERATE *takeaways*

GENERATE is the bright shiny object in the Innovation Universe. The three other foundations—FRAME, EMBED, and LEAD—are in service to GENERATE.

- As a foundation, GENERATE helps you and your leadership team understand the common elements required to create innovations.

- The innovation leaders in your company must make decisions around GENERATE that are not only compatible with your innovation strategy but also harmonize with other initiatives

- The GENERATE elements are iProcess, iMentors, iEcosystems, and iPipe + metrics. These four elements are interrelated; you can't change one without affecting the others.

- iMentors are crucial for innovation from everyone and everywhere. They help your company stay on the leading edge of innovation.

- iEcosystems encompasses the collection of strategic partners, ownership positions, funding, and shared assets that can extend your company's innovation reach.

- iPipe + metrics are critical to track, report, and improve your innovation initiative.

CHAPTER 4

EMBED
Organization renovation

Innovation embedment is just enough to produce pearls
but not so much as to kill the oyster.

If the first foundation, FRAME, is the North Star and GENERATE is the Sun, then EMBED is the Black Hole in the Innovation Universe. It does not have a surface, so it is hard to see. A black hole is a region in space with a vast concentrated mass that fits into an unbelievably small space. Most notably, black holes can collapse on themselves. Black holes have a gravitation pull that is so extreme, even light cannot escape. Ignoring a black hole has dire consequences— in space and in innovation. EMBED, as the black hole of the Innovation Universe, is invisible to all except those who are doggedly looking for it.

I worked with a well-known service company that had a prohibitive nondisclosure agreement (NDA). To a potential partner like me, it seemed like they wanted to lay claim to all of the creative product I had ever produced! In my mind, their one-sided NDA was a "weak signal" about their partnering process. Different from new insights or hard data, weak signals offer a gut check about how difficult it will be for a company to make the shifts needed to become innovative.

I spend much of my time helping companies like this one start or improve innovation initiatives. In advance of my first visit, I prepare by looking and listening for weak signals about the organization's norms, systems, and processes. These pulses are not significant on their own. Yet, when paired with other insights and observations, they offer important clues about the EMBED foundation and whether a company has the open systems and processes in place to innovate.

I experienced another weak signal in the lead-up to a recent engagement with a manufacturing company. We needed a multi-person, multilocation dialogue, and I suggested an online communication app for a virtual meeting. They told me that their company prohibited the use of online communication apps "from the internet," so we made do with a conference call. They did not use technology to enable twenty-first-century collaboration tools; they did everything by landline and fax.

Another company I worked with had what I can only describe as a hairy procurement system. It started with a bidding process for every service, even though their senior leaders had already chosen me for the engagement. Once I cleared that hurdle, the paperwork and documentation were on par with applying for a home mortgage. I should note that this was not a federal contractor or a company that requires vendor security of that nature; this was merely the "way we've always done it." That's all well and good, but when you want to innovate with partners, this procurement system should be viewed as a candidate for renovation.

These weak signals represent protections that were put

in place for a reason, but if the weak signals prove out, I would suggest that they need to be renovated to allow innovation to thrive without losing the protections they provide.

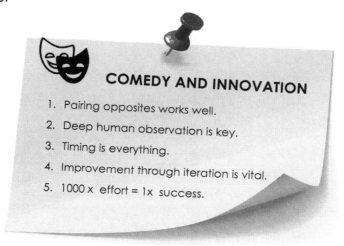

COMEDY AND INNOVATION

1. Pairing opposites works well.
2. Deep human observation is key.
3. Timing is everything.
4. Improvement through iteration is vital.
5. 1000 x effort = 1x success.

Innovation Pivot 12.

Organizational renovation

Management practices put in place before the innovation era helped your company succeed. However, if innovation is to thrive, your company needs to remove barriers and establish innovation-friendly practices and processes. No other foundation orchestrates as much continuous improvement as EMBED, but you need to proceed with care—and avoid bringing the company to its knees as you create change. That is why EMBED calls for a renovation, not a revolution. EMBED is a series of slow, deliberate changes over an extended period of time that will help your company succeed for the next hundred years. Essential for company innovation, EMBED:

- Entails concerted and focused effort.
- Requires someone whom is accountable to help the organization transform.
- Helps establish innovation as a core competency.

The monster in the basement

Think about it this way: your company works day in and day out, even when you are not there. It hums along even when the CEO is on vacation. Something down in the basement is driving it: churning out reports, ensuring compliance, onboarding new employees, taking out cost, enabling predictability, and demanding zero variance. If you are a legacy firm or a company that was not built to be innovative from day one, like so many mature companies, then that thing in the basement is not especially innovation-friendly. We often like to believe that culture is what keeps companies from innovating, but culture is only part of it. EMBED addresses that monster in the basement, including all of its hairy arms and tendrils. EMBED is:

> An ongoing, concerted effort to adapt the company so that innovation is a core competency, long-lasting and always on.

EMBED has four elements that will help you assess and understand which areas to address to bring that monster in the basement onboard for innovation.

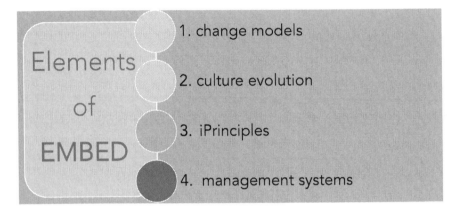

Figure 6. The four elements of EMBED

Evolution, not revolution, is the recurring theme that we see in all of the EMBED elements. EMBED is not about turning the company upside-down in the name of innovation. Instead, EMBED practices slow, gradual change. Four attributes are common in each of the EMBED elements for renovating your organization:

- Make it visible.
- Prioritize the changes using an effort/impact matrix.
- Assign accountability for each change.
- Adapt the selected elements to be innovation-friendly.

If you use the four EMBED elements for organizational renovation to slowly and methodically examine your company, you will be able to adapt your company's internal workings to make innovation a sustainable core competency that comes from everyone and everywhere. It's not easy to renovate an organization but EMBED is the secret sauce you need to make innovation a common cause in your company.

1. Change models

When we envision innovation, we usually think about how it will change the marketplace, customer perspectives, and competitor reactions. We rarely think about how innovation will change our company internally. Yet, as innovation takes hold, significant internal shifts need to occur. We can plan for some of the changes, but others we cannot possibly anticipate. Regardless, companies that avoid change will have a far harder time adapting to become innovation-enabled organizations. *Change models* in the innovation universe are the enterprise and team level change where change models are processes, tools, and techniques in line with iPrinciples. The type of change required within a company as it becomes innovative occurs at two key levels: the enterprise level and the team level.

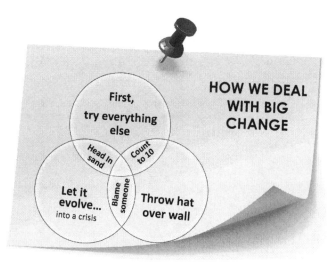

Innovation Pivot 13.

Enterprise-level change

You may believe that your innovation initiative will exhibit steady progress over time, as shown in the "expected" line in the following graphic. However, the universal truth is that enterprise change rarely occurs in a nice, neat progression. In the best case, the "actual" change line progresses up, but then retracts or slows down through a series of switchbacks—usually due to forces occurring elsewhere in the company that have nothing to do with the innovation initiative. The actual progression plays out in a one step forward, two steps back kind of way.

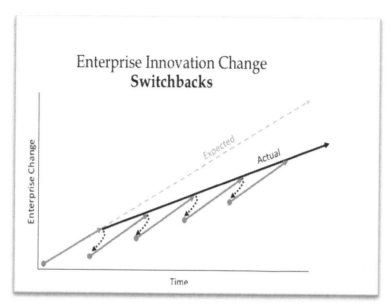

Figure 7.

These dynamics are normal in the life cycle of innovation. Still, if you don't understand the switchback nature of enterprise-level change, you can naturally become frustrated or discouraged. When I started talking about switchbacks in my workshops a few years ago, for instance, I heard audible sighs of relief from participants. After one keynote where I discussed switchbacks, a small group waited for me afterward and said, "You just described our lives!" The good news? Once you understand switchbacks, you can anticipate them and begin to plan how you will pivot in response.

Participants at a workshop I conducted in Copenhagen listed some of the pivots innovation leaders take during their switchback periods. Options vary by company, leader, and the intensity of the switchback, but this is a representative list:

- Mine shelved innovations and see if there is one or two to bring forward.
- Attend external innovation workshops to learn new skills.
- Benchmark other companies.
- Collect learnings from successful and failed innovations and share them.
- Visit new locations in the company to interact with employees on innovation.
- Create the next level of iBlueprint for when innovation is back on the top of the company agenda.

During another workshop, a few participants informed me that they created a professional network with innovation leads from noncompeting companies. One of the benefits of their network is that they "life-coach" and rally around the innovation leader du jour who is stuck in their company's switchback phase.

Another way to think about enterprise change is to envision new innovation initiatives as they progress through an S-Curve of phases from start-up to maturity.

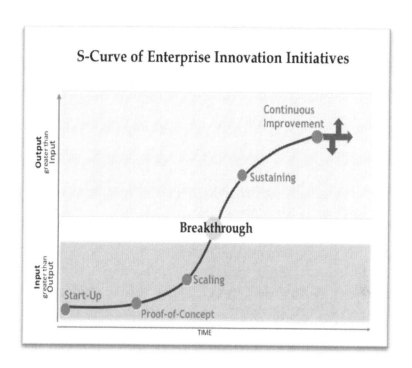

Figure 8.

Your innovation initiative begins at the **Start-Up** phase. Here, guided by your *iBlueprint*, you create the concept for how innovation will work in your company and design the framework for your first innovation teams. The Start-Up phase can take weeks or months, depending on how much alignment you need, how much benchmarking you conduct, how hard it is to allocate resources, and the magnitude of potential innovations.

Next, you put things into play with **Proof of Concept**. This is a living prototype of how innovation teams will organize and progress, but de-risked so you can learn and make improvements as you go. Whirlpool's Proof-of-Concept model was to identify seventy-five employees and train them to be innovators using a common *iProcess* and set of *metrics.*[16] Whirlpool tested its hypothesis with a diverse team using a common set of tools to create core innovations geared to add value for customers.

Things get even more complex in the **Scaling** phase, when you move from a few people to many. To ease the transition, you can use scaling mechanisms such as *iMentors*, definitions, common enterprise *metrics* for innovation projects, and training teams, to name a few. The goal is to expand your innovation initiative from that first innovation team to nearly everyone in the organization.

To the left of the S-curve in Figure 8, you can see that it takes a while for innovations to hit the marketplace. Even after all of these activities, you may still be putting in more resources then you are getting out. In this case, Scaling is when you can expect to find nervous financial types looking over your shoulder and raising red flags about the numbers.

Eventually, you will hit **Breakthrough** and begin to see financial results from your innovations. In this phase, you reach the tipping point where the output from innovation finally exceeds the input. This is when you might decide to take the innovation initiative to the next level with **Continuous Improvement**. For example, if your first S-curve introduced innovation within the core horizons of your company, your second S-curve might expand the initiative to introduce accessories or new-to-the-world horizons. Alternatively, if you started innovating with internal resources, you might develop the muscle to create *iEcosystems* to innovate with strategic partners on the outside.

In some cases, an S-curve takes six months; in others it takes two years or more. It all depends on your company and the factors driving innovation.

The second level of change in the EMBED foundation occurs within an innovation team as it progresses through an *iProcess*. These changes occur equally in large or small teams working on incremental or new-to-the-world innovations. Often the changes are observable only to a trained eye. The innovation team rarely discusses what is happening to them and how they feel about the changes occurring. Again, it is important to realize that the highs and lows are normal.

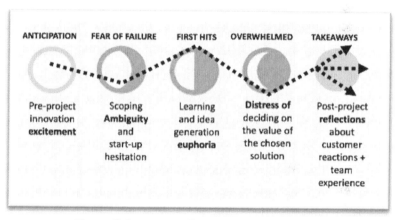

Figure 9. Innovation Team Highs and Lows.

For the most part, people approach innovation projects with high hopes and **Anticipation**. The idea that they will have a chance to innovate is exciting, and they anticipate that the innovation experience will offer a positive change from their normal, routine jobs.

Yet, this inaugural high point is often short lived. In the first phases of any *iProcess*, Anticipation ultimately gives way to ambiguity and innovators, seasoned or not, may experience a **Fear of Failure**. Team behaviors associated with Fear of Failure include holding back good ideas, shutting down, getting cold feet, and the generalized distress that comes with being in a new space with new people and doing new things.

The same changes that trigger Fear of Failure can result in a downward spiral for the team. Helping teams put some structure around their idea and normalizing Fear of Failure (as a typical experience that all innovators share, even it many do not admit it) can help the team roll through the changes. In general, creating safe spaces for them to fail encourages innovators to persevere and offers a way for teams to rise out of these lows.

First Hits create the next innovation high for teams. Hits can materialize by learning from mistakes, interacting with new innovators, and seeing the team's ideas begin to come to fruition. This is a peak moment for most innovation teams. The euphoria that comes with First Hits, and the team changes associated with them, are the stuff of innovators' dreams.

I was working with an innovation team in health care who were innovating the hospital discharge process. If you have been exposed to a hospital discharge process, you know it can be confusing and overwhelming, especially for the elderly. You are frequently left on your own to manage your new reality, including your home and day-to-day life, which may need to be adapted to get you through rehabilitation. Often discharged patients feel that their home is now hostile to their rehabilitation needs. The post-discharge reality may include new physical and social needs, an intimidating new list of medicines and dosages, and doctor and rehab appointment demands that would overwhelm even the best calendaring app.

When the hospital discharge innovation team progressed through the first two phases, Anticipation and Fear of Failure, they started to see connections and ideas that were not available to them when they started. One sub-team used an analog innovation tool where they compared being discharged from a hospital to being discharged from overseas active duty in the military. With that one hit, they started to snowball ideas about how to make discharged patients' new circumstances accepting and enabling for their recovery. As hits progressed, the innovation team started to see articles, posts, and insights about discharge (hospital and military) that before, they would have overlooked. Hits morphed into concepts and prototypes. These First Hits created momentum and confidence for them to transform the hospital discharge process in new and exciting ways.

If First Hits offers the highest of the highs, being **Overwhelmed** is the candidate for the lowest of the lows. A change occurs in innovation teams as they near Launch. This is when panic sets in. Overwhelmed manifests in several ways, represented in these common questions:

- Are we on the right track or is this just a waste of time?
- Will our customers value our solution?
- Did we miss something?
- Can we deliver the solution in the way that we envision it?
- When is it enough and when do we move into Launch?

Being Overwhelmed can arrest team development and send the team spinning into an endless cycle of doubt and distress. If they manage to emerge through these changes, then teams have the chance to bring their innovation to life.

The **Takeaways** are the highs and lows that occur after the innovation project has launched. These insight-driven changes are a result of retrospection by team members about the performance of their innovation and the success of the team. All told, these takeaways have a longer-lasting impact on your innovation initiative than all other team phases put together. If, on the one hand, the teams believe their hard work was worthwhile, and valued by their customers and company, then they will tell that story and it will bolster your company's innovation effort. If, on the other hand, teams feel that their effort was underappreciated and misunderstood, it will be far harder to entice people to join innovation teams at your company in the future.

From a balcony view, the changes that occur at the team level stem from the uncertainty of innovation work, the thrill of offering something new to the world, and the balance teams must walk when they innovate within a company. There are many steps you can take to help innovation teams excel in their highs and mitigate their lows. One avenue to consider is that *iMentors* understand these dynamics and can help teams cope and sustain their momentum as they maneuver through changes.

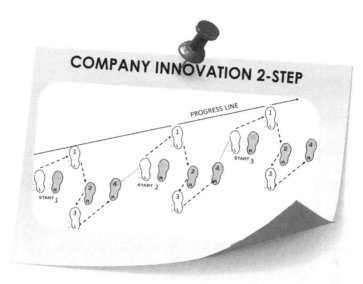

Innovation Pivot 14.

2. Culture evolution

The second element on the EMBED foundation is *culture evolution*—adapting your company's culture to enable innovation.

Corporate culture itself is a system of shared assumptions, values, and beliefs that govern how people behave in organizations. It has a strong influence in the organization and dictates a range of behaviors from how people dress to how they perform their jobs. I entitled this element *culture evolution* because EMBED is not about radical transformation; it is about renovation and slow change. Culture is incredibly difficult to change, especially in long-term legacy companies. However, you can adapt the culture over time and begin to lower the barriers to innovation.

Let's identify a few general descriptors of a company culture that supports innovation:

- Fosters internally driven individuals
- Can both balance the complexity of innovation and pursue it systematically
- Accepting of changes
- Customer-oriented
- Recognizes and values employees as individuals
- Small cross-siloed, diverse innovation teams
- Open communication and collaboration
- Trust and autonomy
- Tolerance of risk-taking and failure
- Patient and far-sighted
- Transparent

When your culture is suboptimal for enabling innovation, where do you begin to create change? The answer is unique to each company, but here are some best practices:

- Start with a few innovation teams. (Don't start with a culture change program, because it will take forever.) Nothing changes the broader culture faster than successful innovations and their teams.
- Launch a few proof-of-concept teams and monitor their progress.
- As innovation teams progress, look for areas that seem to be getting in their way and clear the barriers.

- Sort out whether hard-edged management systems (we will discuss this later) or softer-side culture barriers need addressing.
- Prioritize or triage the first list of culture barriers and determine how you will address them.

In general, people support what they help create. A smart move, then, is to find ways to get people invested in innovation and tip the scales in favor of maximum support. For example, some first-time innovation teams experience a disabling culture barrier if everyone in their organization can "say no." In this case, only the innovation team is invested in the innovation's success, while the rest of the company feels compelled to point out all the reasons why it will fail. If you observe this in your company, one fix is to put some of the prominent nay-sayers on the innovation teams. If the nay-sayers are high up in the organization, consider asking them to become innovation team sponsors. In this case, the sponsors ideally will communicate their positive experience to others in the organization. This, paired with positive results from the first innovation teams, will begin to tip the culture from one where everyone can "say no" to one where supporting innovation becomes the norm.

The competing values framework

Another strategy for nudging *culture evolution* is to take a scientific approach by using one of the many established models that are available. The Competing Values Framework is one that I find particularly beneficial.[17] The framework itself consists of four quadrants that represent organization culture traits. The model exposes "competing values" as the four quadrants push against one another. Although some degree of each quadrant is present in all organizations, every company has a unique Competing Values Profile. The four quadrants are:

- Collaborate: Do things together.
- Compete: Do things fast.
- Control: Do things right.
- Create: Do things first.

An associated diagnostic, the Organizational Culture Assessment Instrument (OCAI),[18] can help identify the areas your company needs to address. I like this assessment because it asks you to describe both the present and the preferred state of culture in your company. I sometimes use the OCAI in workshops to help companies express their culture as it relates to innovation. After participants complete their present and future Competing Values Profiles, I ask them to reach a consensus around the areas of change required to help the company become more innovative.

Culture can be both an enabler and a barrier to your innovation initiative. There are some aspects that you will want to protect at all costs. Consider evolving your culture over time to accentuate the enablers of innovation and reduce the barriers.

Innovation Pivot 15.

3. iPrinciples

One of my first jobs out of college was working for an aluminum company. It had a smelting plant in Louisiana on the banks of the Mississippi River, below the water level in a flood-prone area of New Orleans. In the sign-on documents for every employee at the plant there was a provision that stated, and I'm paraphrasing: *In the event of a flood, all employees must report immediately to the plant to protect it from risk. Those who do not will face termination.* If your home flooded, you were expected to leave it to be at the plant until it was out of harm's way. In this case, the company and its assets came before each employee's family and assets.

It was not *that* long ago that principles guiding how organizations operate required employees to put the company before their personal needs. While this particular draconian policy is likely defunct, other antiquated management principles today drive how companies treat their employees. In the Innovation Universe, you need to challenge outdated management principles and change them into *iPrinciples* to ensure they enable innovation from everywhere and everyone.

Company *iPrinciples* are the underlying guidelines and tenets that inform the collective beliefs and enable (or disable) an innovative organization. While *iPrinciples* may not be as actionable as *change models*, *culture evolution*, or even *management systems* (described below), they are just as instrumental. When they are positive influencers, they can support innovation. If the management principles are unfriendly to innovation, they will impede progress.

As the predecessor to *iPrinciples*, general management principles deserve a closer look. One classic example is the management principles developed in 1916 by Henri Fayol.[19] Fayol, a French executive, author, and contemporary of Frederick Winslow Taylor, is acknowledged as a founder of the modern management method. Having first published his work in France at the tail end of the second industrial revolution, his principles, by all accounts, should be outdated. Yet some of his ideas clearly still govern modern organizations. He described these principles as the underlying factors for successful management. See if you can spot any that still drive management actions in your company:

- Division of Work: Different levels of expertise are distinguished within the knowledge areas (from generalist to specialist).
- Authority and Responsibility: Management has the authority to give orders to the employees.

- Discipline: Obedience is the engine of an organization that runs smoothly.
- Unity of Command: Individual employees should receive orders from one manager and the employee is answerable to that manager.
- Unity of Direction: All activities must be carried out by one group that forms a team. These activities are a plan of action, and the manager is ultimately responsible for this plan.
- Subordination of Individual Interest: Personal interests are subordinate to the interests of the organization.

Another set of common management principles was created by a more contemporary management guru, Peter Drucker. Drucker's principles describe the essential role of managers in this way:[20]

- Sets Objectives: Makes the objectives effective by communicating them to the people whose performance is needed to attain them.
- Organizes: Classifies and divides work into manageable activities and further divides the activities into manageable jobs. Selects people for the management of these units and for the jobs to be done.
- Motivates and Communicates: Performs this integrating function, which forms teams and creates a flow of information.
- Measures: Establishes targets and yardsticks, and analyzes, appraises, and interprets performance.

- **Develops People:** Accentuate this as it takes on even greater importance in the age of knowledge.

As astute as Drucker was and as enduring as his ideas still are, many management principles and "roles of a manager" are outdated in the innovation era. Personally, I don't even like the terms "management" and "manager." They imply all the things we don't want in the Innovation Universe: managers who ensure compliance and micromanage. They suggest that employees cannot be trusted to do their jobs without an "overseer" from the company. Contrast the term "management" and its underlying meaning with what happens in companies that are innovation powerhouses. In the Innovation Universe, these are typical company *iPrinciples*:

- Frame and create a sandbox for innovators.
- Ensure that everyone has access to customers.
- Be open and seek opposing views.
- Experiment for learning, not for perfection.
- Help innovators tap into their passions and emotions.
- Failure leads to insight and learning.
- Seek new perspectives from new entities.
- Co-create with others and look for answers in new places.
- Tell stories to communicate ideas.
- Manage the systems; free the people.

Company *iPrinciples* underlie modern organizations in the innovation age. As with every element on the EMBED foundation, this is not about throwing out all the existing principles. It is about renovating outdated management beliefs to create principles that encourage innovation from every corner of the company.

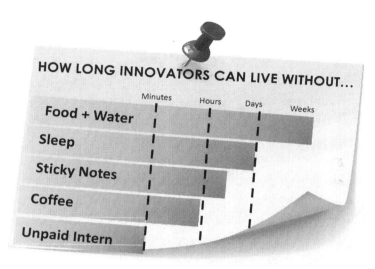

Innovation Pivot 16.

4. Management systems

The best way I have found to understand why *management systems* are so crucial to embedding innovation is to think about your home. Picture yourself in a happy relationship with your significant other. You just moved into your dream home together and it's stunning. Your home is contemporary with clean lines, open concepts, monochromatic calming colors, and a midcentury aesthetic.

You have a staircase that one might see in the iconic smartphone store. There is a kitchen that any chef would envy: premium knives readily accessible in the food preparation area, open shelving with plates under the counter, and a premium cooktop with those enormous knobs to turn on the gas, found at the front for easy reach.

Then a few months later you learn that you are expecting a *baby*.

You look around and realize you are bringing a fragile creature into your home. Your perspective on this beautiful home changes, and now you see danger lurking in every room. You have only a few months to baby-proof your house. You start by putting gates on both ends of the stairs and covers on all the outlets, baby-proofing locks on cabinets and doors, putting medicines out of reach, and changing gas cooktop knobs for safety knobs. If you don't do these things, your dream home will put your baby in danger.

You never go so far as to consider moving. But renovating to make your home safe for your future family?

Absolutely.

The same is true when you bring innovation into your company. In the beginning, innovation is a fragile thing. Some things in your company will endanger innovation—including that monster that lives in the basement. You have to protect innovation and nurture it until it can stand on its own. In the formative years of innovation, you need to protect it by reengineering the management systems that run your company.

Most company's *management systems* were not put in place to allow innovation to thrive. (They most likely predate innovation.) Well-intentioned leaders put them in place to do just the opposite. Your company was built to be predictable, practice zero variance, ensure certainty and repeatability, shun failure, and to keep everything moving on an even keel. Innovation requires the opposite of all that. And in its embryonic or toddler state it will be sacrificed—not through anyone's evil intentions, but by the invisible *management systems* that run your company, day in and day out. Without intervention, most companies have about eighteen months before their innovation programs are slowly and silently shut down. Why? Because their *management systems* are working against them.

I worked with one company that stands out as an apt illustration. When this firm started its innovation initiative, it was a robust, profitable company. Yet, before the senior execs got the program off the ground (and renovated their *management systems*), it was all but impossible to fund innovations in the middle of the budgeting cycle. If you had a great idea and needed a small amount of money, perhaps $25,000, you were out of luck. You had to "find" the money hidden away in someone's budget or wait until the next calendar year to get your project vetted and funded. Since innovation was not yet a core competency, you would likely not get your idea funded with this anti-innovation *management system*.

This is hardly unheard of. In most companies, budgeting systems do not enable innovation; they are not set up to support the unknown, untested ideas that pop up without regard to the fiscal calendar. To circumvent this problem in the short term, Whirlpool established a system whereby seed funds were located close to the ideas.[21] (Seed funds are grants that businesses set aside to fund innovations, usually in small amounts for experiments.) Soon after, Whirlpool adapted its budgeting system to enable funding for innovations on a regular basis. The budget system was not thrown out. Instead, Whirlpool adapted the existing process and turned a barrier to innovation into an enabler.

Management systems are the nearly invisible framework of policies, processes, and procedures used by an organization to ensure that it can fulfill the tasks required to achieve its objectives. They are generally invisible to most people who work in the company. They were likely set up, as your house was before your baby, without innovation in mind. Just as with your house and the budgeting example above, if you want innovation to survive and thrive, don't throw everything out and start over; reengineer your *management systems* to enable innovation.

Management systems guide finance, strategy, operations, human resources, communication, product development, marketing, IT, and space, to name a few. The Management Systems Puzzle gives you a starting point to consider which *management systems* may need reengineering to enable innovation.

Figure 10. Management Systems Puzzle.

Which *management systems* you select to renovate depends on:

- Where you are in your innovation journey
- The unique nature of your company
- How much change your company can tolerate

Companies that believe their culture is derailing innovation fail to realize that often the real culprit is *management systems*. Admittedly, changing them seems like a significant undertaking for companies that feel the innovations themselves should be enough. But failing to renovate *management systems* will cause your company's innovation initiative to struggle, it may even kill it.

EMBED *takeaways*

I was once flying out of Manaus to São Paulo, Brazil. Manaus is the meeting place of the black Rio Negro and the white Solimões River, both tributaries for the Amazon River. From the air, the meeting of the waters was breathtaking, seeing them move together and separate, running side by side. The black river derives its color from the plant and leaf matter that has decayed in the water. The lighter river gets its color from the sediment of the Andes Mountains. The visual separation of black and white is due to the different sources, but also the different densities and water temperatures.

As our plane headed southeast to São Paulo, I could see the rivers flowing side by side for about six kilometers; then they merged in rapids to become the lower Amazon River. Flying over the waters that form the great Amazon River is a once-in-a-lifetime sight.

The same is true for embedding innovation in your company. The norms that have made your company successful have a different source and temperature from those required for innovation, but when they merge, they become an even greater entity. The EMBED foundation will focus on the rapids that combine them, and the actions you take to make innovation part of the water in your company. Here's what to remember:

- The EMBED foundation in the Innovation Universe guides you to renovate your organization so that innovation will work for the long term.

- It is not enough to show that innovation teams can create successful innovations once or twice. You want innovation that is always-on and resident in every job.

- EMBED is a concerted and focused effort that requires someone or some team in your company to be accountable for helping the organization evolve, not only on the hard side of management systems, but also on the softer side of culture evolution and iPrinciples.

- EMBED helps establish innovation as a core competency. What makes it so challenging is that the elements of EMBED are intangible and often invisible to most people in your organization, and they take significant time and effort to address.

- If you want innovation from everyone and everywhere, entrenched in the DNA of your company, the EMBED foundation will help you make the renovations needed to become an innovation powerhouse.

CHAPTER 5

LEAD
Unleashing human potential

The next great space race hinges on attracting leaders who know how to unleash innovation from everywhere and everyone.

Think about any favorite space exploration movie. While the alien settings, hostile environment, and unfamiliar creatures are some of the reasons you love it, what draws you in are the protagonists: the explorers. The story of the space explorer usually follows the hero's arc, based on the amazing work of Joseph Campbell.[22] According to Campbell, the hero's arc includes a call to adventure that takes you away from your home; meeting a mentor; crossing a point of no return; a test, fall, and rebirth; overcoming an ordeal; transformation; a reward; and your return home.

LEAD, the fourth foundation in the Innovation Universe, is not nearly as dramatic as the hero's arc, but the protagonist in this story is a new type of leader all the same. The other three foundations have an organization or project focus, but this one is about *you*. LEAD is how you will thrive in the innovation economy by unleashing human potential, both in yourself and in others. It may not have all the drama of a hero's journey, but it is through leadership that we unleash innovation from everyone and everywhere.

If you want to LEAD in the innovation economy, you'll want to adopt some additional leadership traits to help you and your company succeed. The good news is that for almost everyone, learning and practicing them is fun—nearly as much fun as innovation itself.

Unleashing human potential

Theorists and researchers created many of the classic leadership models in the middle of the last century. Unlike midcentury design, midcentury leadership is not keeping up with workplace trends. To understand the point, consider the following two lists in Table 5. List 1 represents pre-innovation-era workplace trends, while List 2 depicts workplace trends in the innovation era. Imagine how miscast a leader would be using List 1 traits in a List 2 world.

Workplace Trends

Pre-Innovation Era List 1	Innovation Era List 2
• A career with one company is the norm.	• Roles are more attractive than career paths.
• Punch in by 8:00 and leave no sooner than 5:00.	• Unpaid internships provide access to coveted companies and ideas.
• Be at your desk where your supervisor can see you working.	• Freelancers, gig-economy, and start-ups are the norm.
• Job descriptions tell you exactly how to perform your job.	• Working remotely instead of going into the office.
• Supervisors oversee your tasks and time spent.	• Older workforce's use of technology enables working longer.
• You must go through a supervisor to access or interact with an employee in another department.	• Generational work values and practices.
• To show that you have made it, you have an enclosed office with walls, a window, and a door.	• Office spaces are less confining and less structured. Studio spaces.
• Interacting with customers is forbidden; that is the job of the sales department.	• Companies are more social and more casual.
	• Redefining work hours and after-hours requirements.
	• There is less control for the sake of control.

Table 5. Workplace Trends.

Have we altered our understanding of the role of leadership and management as a result of seismic changes in the workplace? Have our underlying leadership models changed to keep up with the reality of social needs and networks within companies?

In my role as an innovation practitioner and teacher, I often work with the sponsors or practitioners who are accountable for innovation within companies. As part of that, I've observed a new set of leadership traits that contribute to far better innovation outcomes. I validated these observations with the current literature on innovation leadership. This led to an Innovation Universe model of leadership, defined as:

> Actuating the innovation economy within your company by practicing, demonstrating, and implementing new leadership traits that enable innovation from everywhere and everyone.

If we think about leaders as the people charged with changing the company so that innovation can thrive, there are two primary roles for leaders in the Innovation Universe.

The first role is to set the conditions and create the appropriate environment for FRAME, GENERATE, and EMBED. This role is easily overlooked by leaders who are drawn to participate in GENERATE as a way to demonstrate their abilities as innovators. (What if J. R. R. Tolkien had become so obsessed with the "precious" that he put down his pen and quit writing to join Gollum's quest to acquire it?) In the innovation economy, the leaders' purview extends beyond participating in innovation. They have additional accountabilities to make their company innovation ready.

The second role of leaders in the innovation economy is to

unleash human potential—in themselves and others. To unleash potential in others means being *in service* to others: teaching, guiding, and investing in their professional growth. To unleash potential in yourself means becoming a student of lifelong learning.

LEAD in the Innovation Universe rests on some new ways of thinking about leadership where leaders' primary value-add is not having all of the answers and controlling people at every turn. Instead, they FRAME the problem, provide the appropriate resources, and equip innovators to find their own answers. As a leader, you are coaching, guiding, and creating inspiring spaces in which innovators can collaborate. You are addressing the organizational barriers so that innovators can thrive. In other words, your role becomes an enabler rather than a controller.

In Gary Hamel and Michele Zanini's latest work, they make a winter storm warming for bureaucracy, and by association for leaders.[23] In the article, they present Haier, the Chinese appliance behemoth, as a collection of microenterprises—new-age business units that have total autonomy to set targets, hire, contract for services such as HR, either inside or outside of the company, seek funding, and structure new and existing businesses to create growth. New leaders are not selected by the talent pool committee as much as they are crowdsourced. If the new leaders don't perform, they are ousted by their teams. This new reality for Haier hinges on more than just leadership; it took Haier a complete transformation to EMBED the systems necessary to get to the point of microenterprises. In the new reality where leaders are crowdsourced and employees become volunteers with discretionary choices, everything we know about leadership is challenged. The Haier story may be a message from the future for leaders. The four elements of LEAD help leaders adopt the new mindset and skill sets for the innovation economy, be it microenterprise or some other incarnation of the new enterprise.

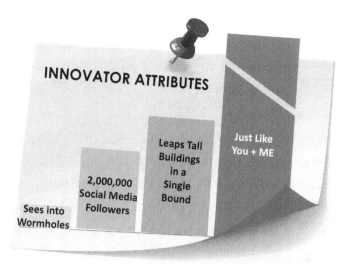

Innovation Pivot 18.

The four elements of LEAD

We will explore four elements in LEAD: network leaders, resource creators, environment architects, and change + thought leaders.

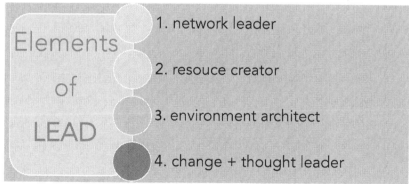

Figure 11. The four elements of LEAD.

1. Network leaders

I had the pleasure of working for Whirlpool for twenty-nine years, the last seventeen as VP of Innovation, reporting to two chairmen and CEOs. In that capacity I traveled the world, meeting with colleagues on innovation topics and visiting innovation teams in their studios. We worked long hours and often ate dinner together or socialized after work. During these after-hours, I found that many of my colleagues had astoundingly creative interests and side projects outside of work. Here is just a sample of their creative talents:

- A director in global finance, one of the most buttoned-up places in any company, was a jazz pianist; his band had two CDs and was working on their third.
- An abstract painter from the IT sold her paintings through her website.
- An engineer who specialized in robotics during the day designed and built furniture in his studio and showed his masterpieces at a local gallery.
- Several designers were part of a Pecha Kucha™ group and excelled at "the art of concise storytelling."[24]
- An executive assistant also had a career in local theater as a professional character actress.
- A marketing professional was also a stand-up comic who honed her set at a local comedy club.
- Others were craft-artisans who sold their creations on a popular e-commerce website.

I realized that there was an undercover network of creatives who engaged in innovative experiences in their spare time. It fascinated me. I wondered if creative types could benefit from knowing and interacting with each other. The thought swirled in my mind and would not go away. I began talking to people about it as a "how might we" question. How might we form a network where like-minded creatives could, on a volunteer basis, socialize and collaborate with each other on an agenda of their choosing?

A few people were attracted to the idea and formed what became the Whirlpool Creatives, a network of over a hundred people who self-organized to help and reach out to one another in our small city. One of the founding members, Chris Gregory, described his first exposure to the Whirlpool Creatives this way:

> The groups of creatives "didn't necessarily work together, but it forced you to sit at this table and realize there's a cross-pollination of skill sets. I didn't know at first all of what it entailed but joined anyway. I don't think I've seen this at any organization I've been at before, which is a big reason why I'm still doing it."[25]

Instead of organization charts or project team charters, *network leaders* look for invisible patterns of interaction that, with a little bit of hosting, could create a valuable experience for members. Networks are voluntary, member-led communities offering a foundation for creative expression, personal meaning, learning, and professional connections.

I distinguish *network leaders* from department managers, as the latter are held accountable for employee productivity. In addition, companies often hold department managers to a full-time equivalent (FTE) number of employees and require them to rate individuals on their performance. Controlling these employees with ratings and incentives is a large part of the department manager's role. Contrast that with the *network leaders*. People in the network don't "report" to the leaders, nor do the leaders evaluate their output. Network members are not in their budget. Instead, the *network leaders* are in service to the network; they help FRAME opportunities that attract members.

Networks unleash human potential and unite like-minded people through exciting social interactions. They are unlike most company-sponsored initiatives and they do not fall under any clear company mandate. You don't control them; you unleash them. Networks are resource attractors, uniting people in pockets of creativity that draw talent to your company. They tap into personal discretionary time and energy, and are owned and controlled by the individual, not the company. Networks are a type of voluntary organization—everyone is there because s/he chooses to be.

With all of that in mind, *network leaders* must learn to attract, curate, and host networks so that members and their company can benefit. The unite constellations of people with shared passions for personal development and innovation using new ways of thinking about talent and the work environment

Networks are a new way of thinking about talent and resources—unleashing rather than controlling, attracting rather than mandating. The support required from your company is minimal. It entails a foundation, so members can find each other, and a small amount of funding to host events. In addition, networks may occasionally require some light support in the form of "air cover," to create a safe space to innovate.

Network leaders take a leap of faith

When you look up at the stars, you see a vast field of lights that appear to have little or no common structure. However, if you understand astronomy or use a celestial guide, you see something entirely different.

Some of us see stars, while others see constellations. *Network leaders* see social network constellations that others miss. They do this through "people" insights: interacting at eye level with individuals who work at the company. They get to know them beyond the role they perform. With some practice, innovation leaders can discern networks that are not apparent to everyone. They understand that these networks would benefit from a hosted format. It's a bit like throwing a party: create a theme, send out invitations, and create a foundation (social gatherings, venues, food and drink, talks, and events), and the people who are interested will show up. The people who get the most out of your parties will continue to attend and bring other like-minded partygoers.

Still, there's no guarantee that a network will take hold or that people will join. Curating and hosting take a leap of faith. It's a little like the feeling Francis Ford Coppola describes in this quote:

> In the middle of filming *Apocalypse Now*, Marty Sheen had a heart attack. For the first time during the making of that picture, I became scared. But we improvised: We used a double and shot a lot of the material from behind . . . To keep going in a crisis, do a 180-degree turn. Turn the situation halfway around. Don't look for the secure solution. Don't pull back from the passion. Turn it on full force.[26]

Uncertain or not, *network leaders* open new vistas for your innovation initiative. After all, networks are part of the secret sauce for pulling resources out of thin air by enabling constellations that others cannot see. Host a great party. Don't look for a risk-free solution and don't pull back. Turn on your passion, full force, and unleash human potential.

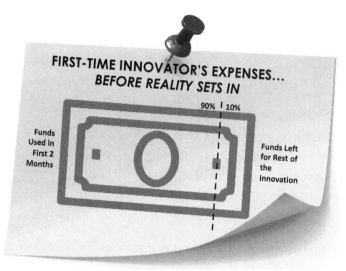

Innovation Pivot 17.

2. Resource creators

Leaders who are *resource creators* contribute to innovation by building a work climate that is a magnet for talent and funding.

The budget orbit

The first way to understand resource creation is by looking at a budgeting cycle within a company. Budgeting is the opposite of resource *creation*—it's resource *allocation*. Here is a typical resource allocation scenario described to me by a senior leader in a large multinational company.

In the fall, the finance group of my company determines the budgets for the next year, based roughly on what each department had the year before, minus some percentage, say 10 percent. At the same time, if you are a department head, you are asked to submit the projects and expenses you are planning for the upcoming year, based on your next year's department goals.

You know the drill: you try to get at least what you had last year. Keep in mind that the company already knows what it's going to allocate to your department; they just haven't told you yet.
You submit your plan; someone cuts it until it roughly meets the 10 percent reduction from what you have in the current year.

You respond by saying that you can't possibly meet your new goals with this reduced budget, but your budget stays unchanged at–10 percent, with increasing levels of expected outputs.

The budgets annually rotate in an orbit where some departments orbit faster, getting more funding, and some slower, getting less. The company decides how much each group will get, and the process repeats year after year. It's nearly impossible to break out of the gravitational pull of the resource allocation orbit that makes you dependent on allocated resources. While resource allocation is a necessary part of your company, think about how it might be adapted to fit in a model with innovation from everyone and everywhere, where ideas can emerge at any time. How can you create an environment where your company supports both resource allocation *and* creation?

In the Innovation Universe, innovation leaders know the power of "and." They use resource allocation as their base; then they expand outward by attracting resources, funding, and people so that they can deliver great innovations.

Turning over rocks

How do you break out of the gravitational pull of resource allocation? *Resource creators* have an unshakable belief that if they come up with a great innovation that will benefit their customers and company, resources will follow. (If you build it, they will come.) They start with the innovation and then work to create resources; they don't wait to receive allocated resources to start innovating. If you want to lead in the innovation economy, your emphasis should be on resource creation.

Resource creators rely on lean approaches to create innovations on a shoestring, the way many great entrepreneurs do. They question every expense and vendor and use their resources to fund small bets. They turn over every rock to find a way to save money. In this case, necessity is the mother of *innovation*.

Resource creators look far and wide for funding. They pitch their idea and generate commitments from inside their company, and then they look outside for strategic partners and investors. Unlike the folklore, they don't start by asking for forgiveness, but they do know how to push the boundaries to get their innovations funded.

After a few successful projects, companies know that *resource creators* will deliver. After that, the company will take greater risks on them than on leaders who are waiting for the mother ship to allocate resources.

Resource creators attract talent much the same way that they attract funding. They create a compelling track record that makes innovators want to work with them. They don't wait for the talent pool committees in the company to allocate people to their teams; they go out and find innovative ways to attract individuals to their cause, from both inside and outside the company.

For many of us, organizational norms lead to a dependent or even an entitled mindset. *Resource creators* never fall prey to that way of thinking; they are self-actualized. If they don't innovate in your company, they will innovate somewhere else. This self-actualization is based on their belief in possibility and their ability to problem-solve. These traits are what turn leaders from budget victims into *resource creators*. Here are some additional traits of *resource creators*:

- Adaptive problem solvers
- Framers + influencers
- Disciples of the lean methodology
- Collaborative mindset
- Possibility thinker
- Does not accept the status quo
- Delights in helping teams find new solutions

I love this quote from Jack Canfield: *Everything you want is on the other side of fear.*[27] That quote comes to mind as we explore leading in the innovation economy, because practicing some of these new traits and behaviors is not about perfecting the status quo, or even improving it. The Innovation Universe encourages you to abandon your comfort zone and adopt new innovation leadership traits.

It takes courage for leaders to get beyond resource allocation and actually create resources to drive their innovations. Over time, they develop a track record of successful innovation that launches a virtuous cycle, bringing them even more funding and talent.

Innovation Pivot 18.

3. Environment architects

Leaders in the Innovation Universe recognize that established companies offer benefits that entrepreneurs in a start-up environment are not privy to, including assets, customers, channels, advertising, and marketing. But innovation leaders understand that these perks come with strings attached, including bureaucracy, inertia, hierarchical mindset, and a status quo that is hostile to innovation. Just as if they were colonizing a planet, leaders in the Innovation Universe need to create a special kind of livable biosphere within their company where innovation can thrive.

A biosphere is an ecological system that integrates people, along with their relationships and interactions, with other environmental elements. The biosphere for the Innovation Universe is not just a physical space; it is also a social one. For innovators to be at their best, this environment needs to be encouraging, safe, and creative. More specifically, it needs to be a learning environment that puts a high premium on addressing customer problems through collaboration and bringing new solutions to market.

Let's take a closer look at several of the characteristics and elements that *environment architects* create in order to unleash the human potential of the innovators in their company.

A safe and engaging space

It may seem alien to some, but many people wait for permission to innovate or even to speak up in meetings and workshops. Some companies have harsh environments or offer little support, so people need a safety net to ideate. If you are looking for innovation from everyone, you don't want only the gifted public speakers to participate in innovation sessions. As a leader, it is your job to make the space safe and engaging.

One of the ways I teach leaders to create such a space is by helping people to say yes. Ask yourself: Can I make it easier for other people to say yes, literally or figuratively?

There are many ways for you as a leader to create safe and engaging spaces, including:

- Developing trust and mutual respect.
- Making sure people understand the strategy sandbox.
- Modeling the innovative behaviors you want.
- Allowing people to work in the safety of pairs.
- Using group techniques that allows participants to work alone first, and then talk.
- Following up every verbal submission with a positive comment or a sincere thank-you.
- Making innovation fun.

Creative spaces

An excellent *Harvard Business Review* article entitled *Collective Genius*, helped me expand my thinking about how innovation leaders practice creative agility as *environment architects*.[28] In these works, Dr. Linda Hill and colleagues talk about innovation leaders who can balance creative agility paradoxes. Their balancing act includes:

- Affirming the individual and the group.
- Supporting and confronting.
- Fostering experimental learning and performance.
- Promoting improvisation and structure.
- Showing patience and urgency.
- Encouraging bottom-up initiatives and intervening top down.

Balancing these creative agility paradoxes helps develop leaders' muscles to become *environment architects* and gives them the tools they need to enable creative spaces, physical and otherwise, where people can innovate.

A place for the whole person

I feel fortunate to work with Dr. Harry Davis of the University of Chicago. In his classes, he discusses the need to "bring your whole person to work." This whole-person acceptance, of both yourself and others, is a crucial trait of leaders who want to architect spaces for innovators to thrive. An excellent article by Stewart Friedman from Wharton, entitled "Be a Better Leader, Have a Richer Life," captures the whole-person idea in what Friedman calls Total Leadership.[29] Friedman's concepts do something that most theories do not—they provide a call to action to experiment by changing your life and considering how that change can benefit four domains of our lives: work, home, community, and self. Friedman points to the whole person and underscores that we are richer when we don't compartmentalize ourselves. He teaches us to see that a change for the better in one domain can affect other areas of our lives as well.

Friedman's steps for leading whole-person change include:

- Experiment with describing goals in each of the four areas.
- Implement steps to make the change.
- Adjust and assess your outcome.

Friedman's work represents one of many schools of whole-person leadership. The bottom line is that innovation leaders bring their whole selves to work and help others do the same in an authentic and positive way.

Leaders who listen and encourage

Derived from an improvisation technique, the idea of "Yes, and" epitomizes the environment required for innovation.[30] The basic premise for "Yes, and" is that when you hear an idea, you accept it without judgment. You then throw it back to the idea creator with an affirmative response (*Yes*), while adding something new that builds on the idea (*and*). Imagine that you finally get up the courage to go to your boss with a wildly creative idea for the business, and instead of saying "We already tried that" or "No one asked you for that idea," she accepts it and tosses it back over to you along with a nod to keep working on it.

There is a 24-carat question that innovation leaders can use to encourage innovation teams to new levels. It cleverly implies "Yes, and," but it goes one step further by asking, How might we make this work? The question is How Might We? It offers the idea creators an affirmative space and opens a door for them while asking them to take accountability for executing their idea so that it will work.

While "Yes, and" can help us collaborate to develop new ideas, How Might We? allows teams to come up with solutions. Adding How Might We? to your lexicon will help you architect environments that bring out the best of innovators.

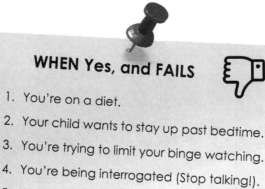

WHEN Yes, and FAILS

1. You're on a diet.
2. Your child wants to stay up past bedtime.
3. You're trying to limit your binge watching.
4. You're being interrogated (Stop talking!).
5. When ideas are stupid/stupid not smart/stupid.

Innovation Pivot 19.

Generativity

Generativity is a concept coined by psychoanalyst Erik Erikson as part of his eight stages of adult personality development.[31] The generativity stage is when we "make our mark" on the world by creating or nurturing things that will outlast us as individuals. Each of Erikson's stages has a virtue associated with it. In this case, the virtue is care. Generativity is when we start giving back by teaching and becoming involved in our communities.

Similarly, great leaders give back as they work with others to bring new innovators along. They are beyond needing to be the smartest person in the room, and they don't need to compete with everyone. When innovation leaders are generative, they seem to be at peace with themselves. They focus on helping others reach their innovation potential. Generative leaders see the best in people and want to unleash their potential. Imagine working for someone this grounded, generous, and caring. If you want to attract resources as an *environment architect*, generativity is a leadership trait you will develop.

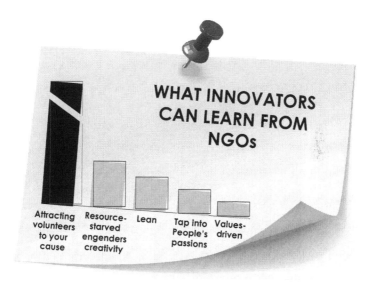

Innovation Pivot 20.

Leaders who are regenerative

In electric cars, regenerative braking systems turn the kinetic energy created from braking into heat that helps recharge the car. In this case, the energy is not only recycled but also improves the performance of the vehicle.

In leadership, someone who is regenerative takes everything—a meeting, idea, or system—and makes it better. This goes beyond "Yes, and," which sends the idea back to the creator for additional development. Regenerative describes leaders who take the energy that exists around an idea or solution and use it to take the idea to the next level.

I watched a regenerative leader work his magic on an innovation team at Whirlpool in the early days of innovation at the company. This was a product team whose members saw themselves as creating washers and dryers. They innovated under that point of view: we make and sell washers and dryers. The regenerative leader worked with the team for many weeks, helping them expand their thinking without giving them the answer. He kept asking them: How big can this space be? Ultimately, they moved from conceptualizing washers and dryers to thinking about optimizing the laundry process within the home. It may sound like a mere nuance to go from washers and dryers to laundry optimization, but it was not. Because of this regenerative leader who patiently and continually asked the innovation team to explore how big their space could be, Whirlpool forever changed the way it thought about bundled and connected solutions for customer processes within the home.

Regenerative leaders are always looking for possibilities. They also are nonjudgmental and view the situation as a glass half full. As leaders, helping others get their idea or career to the next level is paramount for creating an environment where people want to innovate.

In fact, people want to work for leaders who are regenerative.

Like "Yes, and" leaders and those who practice whole-person leadership—as well as the other elements mentioned above—this is yet another trait that will help you be the architect of an environment that attracts innovators and becomes a hotbed for new solutions that customers love.

4. Change + thought leaders

Across the Innovation Universe, leaders are change agents who understand the transformation that is required to make innovation work. They become *thought leaders* within innovation, where they help others move from innovation platitudes to specific knowledge about innovation.

For your company to become truly innovative, someone needs to step up and lead the changes and renovations required in FRAME, GENERATE, and EMBED. Before we review the Innovation Universe Leadership Model, let's look at the role of leaders as *change leaders* in the other three foundations, and as *thought leaders*.

FRAME change leader

The change agent task in FRAME calls on you to create and communicate a strategy that frames innovation as a critical driver of company results. It is essential to ensure that innovators in your company have the context they need to innovate. They also need to understand the clear connection between strategy execution and what they do in their everyday work.

If you are leading the innovation initiative or an innovation team, FRAME elements may technically be someone else's responsibility. In reality, companies do not always fulfill their responsibilities around this task. Your leadership role in FRAME is to fill in the gaps and help your innovators recognize how their innovations contribute to company success.

GENERATE change leader

Leaders get tripped up in the GENERATE foundation when they believe their role is to create the next great innovation as opposed to making innovation possible from everyone and everywhere. As a leader on the GENERATE foundation, you need to help your company decide on the *unifying iProcess* so that all innovators are on the same page and using a common language. You need to create the *iEcosystems* where innovators spend their time. You can also bring in *iMentors* or facilitators as a way to help innovation teams track and measure their success.

Your other change-related leadership role in GENERATE is to provide air cover for innovation teams. By their nature, innovation teams dust up controversy and make organizations uncomfortable. As a *change leader*, you need to give innovation teams the support to allow their ideas to germinate.

EMBED change leader

The change-leadership role in EMBED is a bit more nuanced. First and foremost, you need to train yourself in the elements of EMBED so that you can see the underlying systems and dynamics that drive your company. As you mentor and unleash innovation teams, you need to stay close enough to them to understand the organizational barriers they are facing. (Often, innovation teams cannot see the barriers themselves; it takes someone with the right leadership lens.) Keep a running list of the management systems and begin to triage the ones that need renovation.

If all else fails, be sure that you are practicing the EMBED elements in the area you manage. You might not be able to change the whole company, but you can begin in your business unit, department, or team.

In addition to leading the changes required in FRAME, GEN-ERATE, and EMBED, *thought leaders* in the Innovation Universe are informed, educated, and experienced in one or more aspects of innovation. They are the trusted guides who help and inspire people with information and practitioner advice concerning their areas of innovation expertise. Expertise and knowledge are what differentiates *thought leaders* from those who trumpet innovation platitudes.

I advise leaders to take one aspect of innovation that you are passionate about and master it. The innovation space changes daily, making it almost impossible for anyone to be an expert in all facets. That makes it easier to put your toe in the water of innovation knowledge, and to keep yourself abreast of new ideas in innovation by reading, attending workshops, taking classes, and putting yourself in networks where you can learn and grow.

One of the best ways I know to master an area is to write about it and/or teach it. The reality is that too many leaders in innovation don't have the baseline knowledge they need, so they get by on platitudes and buzzwords. Leaders in the Innovation Universe go deep and become *thought leaders* in one or more aspects of innovation.

The Innovation Universe leadership model

The Innovation Universe Leadership Model outlines the critical abilities that go beyond your basic leadership skills to help you lead in the innovation economy. I encourage you to review the table below and identify one trait that you can commit to improve in yourself to become a better Innovation Universe leader.

The Innovation Universe Leadership Traits

Adaptive problem solver	Addresses previously unsolved problems by using new learnings and deep customer insights and by overturning orthodoxies. Compassionately helps innovation teams thrive in disequilibrium.
Generative	Teaches and guides the next generation. Creates offerings that make the world a better place. Gives back and fosters the common good.
Regenerative	Actively improves ideas, places, and systems through collaboration. Practices a "Yes, and" leadership approach and looks for possibilities. Humanity ethnographer.
Whole-person learner	Maintains an active, ongoing, and self-sustaining pursuit of knowledge and personal development through the whole person: mind, body, and spirit.
Creatively agile	Has the ability to generate ideas through debate, test and experiment, and make integrative decisions that combine opposing ideas.
Resource attractor + creator	Attracts talent, time, and funding through generative and regenerative approaches. Creates a destination workplace for innovators.
Social architect	Creates open, safe, and engaging "spaces" for all people to contribute, feel valued, and vote with their feet. Pushes on systems; frees innovators.
Frames + influences	Creates a sandbox for innovation to optimize limited resources. Influences others to collaborate and arrive at the best outcome, using a lean approach.
Curates collaborative teams + networks	Taps into the discretionary resources while ensuring commensurate rewards. Builds collaborative teams and unlocks social networks for the sake of personal and organizational growth.
Communicates at eye level	Hosts transparent and engaging dialogue with others to help them become better innovators; treats them as equals.

Table 6.

I have been fortunate to work with many great innovation leaders. They have mentored me and challenged my thinking on what it takes to lead innovation. Great innovation leaders fall under the element of *you know them when you see them*. There is something about them—you want to be around them, learn from them, and impress them. Their aura envelops innovation teams and they create spaces where teams are at their best.

Many of the leadership models that we still use in organizations are holdovers from the last century, derived prior to the innovation era. Leaders in the Innovation Universe develop leadership traits and behaviors around the four elements of LEAD that are in concert with the innovation era: *network leaders, resource creators, environment architects*, and *change + thought leaders*.

The good news is that we are all relatively new to the Innovation Universe. In the annals of management theory, innovation is barely a toddler. Our companies are unique enough that there is no one-size-fits-all approach to leading innovation. We are learning together to transform our basic leadership abilities into leadership skills in the Innovation Universe so that we can unleash human potential at every turn.

LEAD *takeaways*

LEAD is the Innovation Universe foundation that focuses on you. It helps you identify and adopt new leadership roles and traits that are crucial for your company's innovation effort, and for you to become a leader in the innovation era.

- LEAD entails actuating the innovation economy within your company by practicing, demonstrating, and implementing new leadership traits that enable innovation from everywhere and everyone.

- Leaders have two primary roles in the Innovation Universe. The first is to set the conditions that create the appropriate environment for FRAME, GENERATE, and EMBED. The second is to unleash human potential in themselves and others.

- Network leaders look for invisible patterns of interaction that, with a little bit of hosting, could create a valuable experience for members. Networks are voluntary, member-led communities offering a foundation for creative expression, personal meaning, learning, and professional connections.

- Resource creators build a work climate that is a magnet for talent and funding. Leaders use resource allocation as their base and expand outward by attracting resources, funding, and people, so that they can deliver great innovations.

- Environment architects create encouraging and creative learning environments that put a high premium on addressing customer problems through collaboration and new solutions.

- Leaders understand the transformation that is required to lead within innovation, where they help others move from innovation platitudes to specific knowledge about innovation.

CHAPTER 6

Practitioner wisdom:
Starting and improving
innovation

Colonize the Innovation Universe to transform your company into an innovation juggernaut.

Have you ever watched one of those suspense movies where the thief engages in amazing acrobatic feats to avoid tripping a laser security alarm? Remember Tom Cruise in *Mission Impossible*, suspended from the ceiling like a spider? Or the most choreographed thief scene ever, with Catherine Zeta-Jones doing a laser-beam-evasion dance under the watchful eye of Sean Connery in *Entrapment*? The laser beams are everywhere and it's tricky...one misstep and the prize is gone.

Breaking ground for innovation is like that laser-beam-evasion dance, although not as entertaining. If you are the leader charged with embedding innovation in an organization, the cultural, bureaucratic, and systemic barriers are like hundreds of laser beams all around you, and the danger of tripping the alarm is intense.

Practitioner wisdom

I build unstructured time into my innovation workshops to talk about what is on the minds of the practitioners. Some, including recently minted innovation leads, have that look of sheer terror in their eyes. (I remember that feeling from when I was in their shoes.) Invariably, these interactive discussions center on *How would you start this program if you were me?* In the same workshops, we also have innovation practitioners with more experience under their belts. These conversations, although just as urgent, revolve around *How I can boost my current innovation approach and take results to the next level?*

What lessons have I gleaned from all of these discussions and interactions? *A lot.* There is a great deal of practitioner wisdom out there, and I've made it my mission to capture it.

In fact, I will use examples of that accumulated practitioner wisdom to drill down on the two scenarios mentioned above. First, I will unpack practitioner wisdom that can be applied when companies are ready to launch an innovation initiative from scratch. In this case, practitioners are invariably using a lean start-up approach and don't have a lot of time or money to get going. As usual, someone in the C-suite is leaning on them to show results. Still, they don't wait until everything is perfect; their goal is to get started and adapt or pivot as they go. This section is about innovation initiative start-up ideas and cautions.

Next, we will extract and apply practitioner wisdom for instances when experienced leaders need to take their innovation initiative to the next level. Each company is different, of course, so there is no one-size-fits-all approach. Still, we will explore several solutions that can help you overcome barriers, dodge the laser beams, and put continuous improvement into practice. In these cases, the practitioner wisdom comes from companies whose innovation initiative was already in orbit, and they experimented with savvy ways to boost performance. This section focuses on the continuous improvement required to get your existing innovation initiative to the next level.

Both scenarios will prove relevant for any organization making its way across the four foundations of the Innovation Universe. In addition to ideas in each area, I've included one practitioner warning as an example of where things can go wrong.

Start-up

In our start-up scenario, practitioner wisdom points us to three types of enablers you can use to create a path for innovation: Setup Tools, First iTeams, and Start-up Accelerants.

START-UP	
Practitioner Wisdom	
Setup Tool	• Form a core team • Sandbox and domains • Types and approaches • Innovisits • Innovation luminaries • Practitioner warning
First iTeams	• Supporting iTeams • T-1 engagement survey • Resource plan • Practitioner warning
Start-Up Accelerants	• iNetwork • Customer results • Senior leader events • Practitioner warning

Table 7.

Innovation leaders often need to launch programs quickly without the benefit of abundant resources. The following ideas form a toolkit of lean thinking to help you get off the ground in a fast and frugal way.

Form a Core Team. One of the most essential tools for launching innovation in your company is a core team of people who will guide the innovation initiative. Ideally, this small team should include influencers and other individuals with enough clout in the company to help you attract funding and support. As part of that, always include a communicator to help you tell your story, and a finance person to track and report key performance indicators (KPIs). In general, find kindred spirits. (If these kindred spirits have some discretionary money in their budget, even better.) Keep your core team small: three or four people you "borrow" for three months to help in the start-up phase of innovation.

Define Your Sandbox and Domains. You will not succeed without a sandbox, which is the defined space in which you will innovate and experiment. Within that sandbox, innovators carve out chunks of real estate called domains, which are the customer areas they will explore for their innovation. Be smart about choosing your first domain. If your company makes cars and your first teams work on, say, the next men's razor, no one will care. Make sure the domain is large enough to allow the first teams to breathe, and small enough to generate a win—but not so small that it won't prove the case for innovation.

Decide on Types and Approaches. Determine the types and approaches for the first wave of innovations. For instance, you may want to start in with core innovation and then move to adjacencies. Or you could start with innovation projects in one business group and then scale them to all groups. You may want to start with an innovation garage and then move innovation into every business unit in your company. Most practitioners recommend starting in a controlled experiment to prove the case for innovation.

Requesting Your Company to Fund an Innovation Studio Before Your First Innovation Result Is Like:

Requesting	Before
A Tip	Serving Dining Customers
An IPO	A Track Record of Success
20 Weeks' Vacation	Starting a New Job
Accolades on Your Novel	Writing It

Innovation Pivot 21.

Schedule Innovisits. Innovisits are outreach trips where people from your company call on noncompetitors to learn about their innovation initiative.[32] Many companies are very willing to open their doors for this short, targeted benchmarking excursion. To make the most of an innovisit, use the Innovation Universe framework to select the areas where you most need help, such as selecting an *iProcess*. Find two companies that are using the *iProcess* you are considering and schedule a half-day visit. Invite people from your company to come—either those who can help you get started or others who might be converted to your cause by a behind-the-scenes look at an innovative company.

Practitioner wisdom suggests bringing a small gift as a gesture of gratitude. In addition, as your program grows and progresses, return the favor by hosting companies that are trying to get started or are looking for specific learning.

Invite an Innovation Luminary. If you have the budget, invite an innovation luminary to host a short workshop or keynote for your senior leaders. The luminary can be an innovation *thought leader*, a respected CEO, a chief innovation officer, a leader from an innovative company, an academic, or a consultant. Make sure the person has at least one great story, relevant to your business, about a notable innovation that took off. It's helpful if there are some similar traits to your company. For example, if you are a B2B company, make sure the luminary has B2B examples.

Setup Practitioner Warning. Within your defined domain, decide if you will mine ideas that are already kicking around the company or allow teams to propose original ideas. Practitioner wisdom recommends that you respect existing turf and start with original ideas. This clean slate approach keeps you free of legacy biases or political land mines. If some ideas are already in the ether, put a process together to evaluate them against the sandbox, but do this only after your first teams complete a cycle.

First iTeams

Abiding by a few proven best practices will give your first iTeams their best chance for success. This practitioner wisdom gives teams what they need to get started and attract other leaders and employees to the innovation cause.

Structure and Socialize iTeams. Form two or three iTeams to work within the first domain. As part of that, choose a business leader from the domain (ideally an innovation kindred spirit) as the iTeam sponsor. You can organize the iTeam in a cross-functional or cross-element way if that particular structure fits the problem to be solved. In the first round, practitioner wisdom recommends keeping the iTeam internal, without introducing outside partners or innovators unless they are uniquely qualified to help you get the process going. Situate the iTeam in an open area, near the cafeteria or other high-traffic destination, so people can see them as they walk to get coffee or go to meetings. You need to spend time with the first iTeams—there is no substitute for front-line knowledge of their experiences and what might be holding them back, especially in the early months of the start-up.

Conduct an Engagement Survey. If time permits, conduct a short pulse survey that targets a broad population of company employees. (You can use one of the inexpensive, online survey options.) The objective is to create a "before" picture of your organization, so that as you progress and innovation starts to take hold, you can use engagement figures as one of your input *metrics*. Practitioner wisdom suggests survey questions such as these:

- Do most of our employees understand innovation and how it works?
- Do employees feel our company is innovative?
- Do they have ideas for innovation, and do they feel able/empowered to explore and develop these ideas?

Create a Resource Plan. Secure enough funding and resources to support the first iTeams in the first budget cycle. If you start midcycle, piece together the funding to get started. You should use lean principles for financing—that is, do everything fast and on the cheap. Remember that time- and resource-starved innovation teams can funnel their ingenuity to achieve amazing things. Establish one or two KPIs that you will use to assess the first innovations and their results (financial or otherwise). Make sure your KPIs include customer measures and other metrics that senior leaders will support.

One First-Teams Practitioner Warning. If teams are working on innovation full time for some defined period, have a clear and specified path to where they will go after the innovation iTeam concludes. Employees will be more willing and eager to sign on as the first innovators if they know what is next for them. One practitioner addressed post-innovation assignments with this wisdom:

- Some innovators stay on to work on the innovations that progress to become new businesses in the company.
- Other innovators will become iMentors.
- The rest of the team will return to their previous roles (make sure this is agreed to before the iTeams are chosen) with a more profound understanding of business and innovation that the company will value as innovation progresses.

Start-up accelerants

Valuable practitioner wisdom can help accelerate your progress once the first iTeams are off and running. The next sections offer some of some of the most useful practitioner wisdom of all.

Create an Innovation Network. Start a self-led iNetwork of about ten innovation zealots. Give them articles or books to read, take some of them on innovisits, and include them in discovery and ideation efforts to add an "outside" perspective. Tap into them when you need help and use them for support and inspiration.

Collect Customer Results. Collect customer feedback and use it to develop and improve the solutions your customers need most. There may be a period when you and the iTeams know more about your customers than anyone in the company. Use that knowledge to make the case for why innovation should be scaled to everyone.

Present at Senior Leader Events. If your company has senior leader events and meetings, arrange for teams to use those forums to present their work and gain visibility for innovation. Help them prepare but allow them to tell their story in their own words. Nothing sells an innovation initiative better than passionate, customer-centric, knowledgeable, creative, and diverse innovators who tell the tale of their exciting and rewarding innovation journey.

Accelerate Practitioner Warning. Having iTeams interact directly with customers may threaten the groups that traditionally serve as the customer advocates within the company. In many companies, these may be the market research, marketing, or sales teams. To convert this potential negative into a positive, consider adding one or two members from these groups as extended or even core iTeam members.

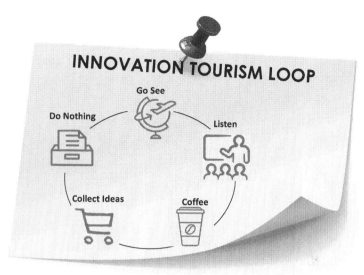

Innovation Pivot 22.

Continuous improvement

It may seem like an oxymoron, but innovation is a continuous improvement challenge. You will find that once your innovation initiative gets to a particular plateau, you become dissatisfied because you know that you can do even better. This is a key trait of all healthy and growing innovation initiatives— you are *perpetually dissatisfied*. This is a good thing. As a result, many companies find that they need a plan every two or three years to help boost innovation to the next level.

Note, however, that practitioner wisdom pertaining to continuous improvement is harder to generalize than start-up wisdom. Why? Because companies at this advanced stage have customized their innovation initiative to suit their unique needs. Ideally, the practitioner wisdom below can be widely applied by looking at it in the levels that I describe as follows:

Deeper, addressing learning; *Faster*, addressing leveraging, and *Wider*, addressing scaling.

Deeper: Learning	• Knowledge centers • Gaming • Innovation showcase • Topical talks • Practitioner warning
Faster: Leveraging	• Content expert registry • Exchange *iMentors* • Sponsors • Create synergies with OpEx • Practitioner warning
Wider: Scaling	• Partner with your installed base • Social innovations and NGOs • Migrate innovation tools • Practitioner warning

Table 8.

Deeper: Learning

Deeper is how you increase the organization and team learning by acting in ways that help your company to go deeper into the innovation space.

Create Knowledge Centers. Establish an online repository for innovation-relevant information and insights to position innovation as a shared resource for learning. Areas to focus on in innovation knowledge centers include competitors, customers, megatrends, innovation developments, discontinuities, and emerging technologies.

Use Gaming to Train. Another deeper action that many companies have used to drive innovation is training. In some cases, organizations use tools such as massive open online courses (MOOCs), where everyone goes online for training on the same day. This gets basic innovation knowledge out to all employees and creates an innovation esprit de corps. As part of this, you can create a gaming environment around training that inspires people to learn more and get involved.

Establish an Innovation Showcase. Many companies establish ways they showcase innovations from employees and partners. For instance, they may create a one-day event where innovation teams tell their story on stage. Companies often add an educational component to showcases so that everyone at the event is learning something new about innovation. Events like this work best when they are celebratory, lauding the effort and passion of fellow innovators.

One company I work with creates large events where they invite employees, suppliers, and commercial partners. It has become so large and popular that each year they rent a professional football stadium to host the events.

Topical Talks. Start internal "topical talks" to explore and share intelligence about all aspects of innovation. Invite partners and innovators to present on areas of interest. This is an excellent opportunity to bring colleagues in from other companies to talk about common areas of interest around innovation.

Deeper: Practitioner Warning. Don't get distracted, spread yourself too thin, or move too far from the core of the innovating effort. These deeper learning practitioner wisdom ideas are intended to show how one or two actions may be enough to generate the continuous improvement required to take your innovation initiative to the next level.

Innovation Pivot 23.

Faster: Leveraging

Practitioner wisdom on the topic of faster focuses on how to leverage what is already in your company to help you leap-frog to the next level.

Create a Content Expert Registry. Starting a registry with the names and email addresses of content experts in your organization gives iTeams fast, easy access to internal expertise. For example, one company that manufactures railroad parts included metallurgists in its registry. Another, a product company, included designers and market researchers. Think about the deep expertise that exists in your company and create a resource, with permission from the experts, to help iTeams leverage the skills that exist in the organization.

Exchange *iMentors*. Instead of payrolling more *iMentors* than you need, create an *iMentor* network with companies that are using similar tools and *iProcesses*. This demonstrates an efficient use of resources and allows you to partner with *iMentors* who have exposure to many different companies, *iProcesses*, and business models.

Invite Executives as Sponsors. Consider inviting senior leaders to sponsor iTeams. Executive-level sponsors can mentor iTeams and help them bypass barriers. The hidden benefit is that senior leaders who witness innovation are in a better position to leverage it in other areas of the company.

Create Synergies with Operational Excellence. Pair your innovation tools with tools from Six Sigma to create a comprehensive problem-solving methodology. While you are at it, take stock of other critical business initiatives and their tool kits to give employees simple problem-solving steps that come from the best that innovation and continuous improvement can offer. You might create a five-step problem-solving methodology that every employee can use to solve everyday problems using tools from innovation and Six Sigma. For example:

- Step 1: Frame the problem, using innovation tools.
- Step 2: Go deeper to understand the problem, using Six Sigma analytic tools or innovation customer empathy tools.
- Step 3: Create ideas for solutions, if new-to-the-world ideas are needed, using innovation tools; if efficiency or compliance ideas are needed, use Six Sigma tools.
- Step 4: Run experiments to test solutions, using design of experimentation tools from Six Sigma.
- Step 5: Assess, improve, and share.

Faster: Practitioner Warning. Keep senior leaders in the loop about iTeam efforts and ongoing innovation initiative progress. As tempting as it may be to fly under the radar, shutting out executives is dangerous and shortsighted. It is dangerous because executives who feel blindsided may either withhold their support or actively work to shut down illicit efforts to innovate. It is shortsighted because senior leaders have skills, contacts, and experience that iTeams can use to help them remain focused and appropriately aligned with the larger business strategy. Once they have bought into the power of innovation, it is often these same senior leaders who have the best ideas about how to take the program to the next level.

Wider: Scaling

Scaling is a particularly substantial challenge along the way to creating innovation from everywhere and everyone. Once you prove the concept of company-wide innovation, practitioner wisdom provides some ideas for scaling mechanisms that can help you recruit more people to the task of creating robust innovations aimed at current and future customers.

Partner with Your Installed Base. If you started innovation inside your company, scaling concepts to *iEcosystems* will help you deliver new-to-the-world innovations. One of the best first steps in open innovation is to partner with companies you are already working with: commercial partners, existing collaborators, vendors, and suppliers. If you have *iMentors*, they will be a competitive advantage here as the partners will value a facilitated process for the joint innovation.

Partner with Social Innovators and NGOs. If your company has a significant social responsibility initiative in the communities in which you operate, consider scaling innovation tools with NGOs in mind. Often the problems that NGOs face—programming, sufficient volunteers, donations, and marketing, to name a few—can be solved using innovation tools. This gives innovators a chance to use their tools in new ways while they help NGOs in their community. It is also an excellent chance for *iMentors* to learn new applications and explore business models that may be helpful in future company innovation sessions.

Migrate Tools to Create Innovations. Add innovation tools such as migration maps, storytelling, or value proposition to leadership development, recruiting, performance evaluations, functional training, and problem-solving workshops. Scaling these types of tools and getting them out into the company is part of casting a wide net so that innovation tools are available to all employees who can leverage them in new and value-adding ways.

Use learning maps to create fun and educational experiences for all employees. A learning map is a graphic that depicts and simplifies a subject that you want employees to learn, and then adds a series of lessons or steps to map the experience in a fun and interactive way. Train learning map facilitators and host one to two-hour open-enrollment events for all employees to learn more about innovation. Give a fun prize for showing up. Videotape the event and put it on your employee website. There are many excellent vendors who create learning maps, including Root Learning, the company we used at Whirlpool.[33]

One year at Whirlpool we had a balanced scorecard item to train every salaried person on the fundamentals of innovations and their role in learning innovation. We created an e-learning course and hosted it on our learning management system for the twenty thousand employees. Completing the course was an objective on their annual performance appraisal. Today there are many ways to host e-learning courses that are accessible and inexpensive to offer to all employees. You can't teach innovation online, but you can establish a fundamental baseline of understanding through e-learning.

Wider: Practitioner Warning. One danger to avoid is accelerating to try *wider* ideas before you have your innovation initiative grounded and stable. Ensure that you have a track record of success before you invite your strategic partners into your innovation studio.

Practitioner wisdom *takeaways*

Innovation is a collaborative discipline. We all achieve better results working together in diverse teams, sharing lessons and insights, casting a wide net with teams and sponsors, and looking for ways to keep innovation open and transparent. In my own experience teaching, coaching, and consulting within organizations, I have found that some of the best insights on innovation come from practitioners who have acquired knowledge through blood and sweat equity. Even more, I found that they are willing to share their wisdom to help enable innovation from everywhere and everyone.

In this section, we looked at practitioner wisdom for the start-up stage: creating a core team, staking out an innovation sandbox and domains, identifying types and approaches, engaging in innovisits, and inviting luminaries to speak are a few of the tools innovators can use to get set up.

- The first iTeams can gain traction by socializing their goals, creating resource plans, and tracking engagement metrics.

- Creating iNetworks, tracking customer results, and presenting innovation at executive events can help accelerate support for innovation at the start-up phase.

- We also examined practitioner wisdom aimed at helping innovators scale new heights.

- Building knowledge centers, using gaming for training, and trying innovation showcases and topic talks all provide deeper learning to increase internal support and help innovation initiatives grow.

- Setting up expert registries, exchanging iMentors, inviting executive sponsors, and creating synergies with operational excellence are ways to leverage existing company assets to grow innovation programs faster.

- Scale innovation by partnering with your installed base, expanding to serve NGOs, and using migration tools.

The Innovation Universe ®

FRAME | GENERATE | EMBED | LEAD

GENERATING + delivering a cadence of unique + value-creating solutions for customers, while FRAMING + LEADING innovation as a core competency, EMBEDDED in every aspect of your company.

FRAME: *The Strategic Mandate*

A clear and understood enterprise or business unit strategy that requires innovation and includes why, who, where, how much, and when as well as the linkages and benefits from innovation for the company and its customers.

1. Strategic Architecture	2. iBlueprint	3. Definition + Criteria	4. Structure + Fit
Alignment of enterprise vision, mission, strategies, goals, and values.	Strategy for the innovation initiative, aligned with the business strategy.	Definition provides the description of the unique innovation qualities required for customers to consider a product or service innovative. Criteria allow companies to classify and count innovations.	*Structure* refers to how you organize your innovation effort. *Fit* addresses how your company deploys innovation with other key initiatives from your strategy.

GENERATE: *Customer-Driven Problem Solving*

The process and methods used to develop innovations, from insights to commercialization, that are valued by the customer. Bringing a cadence of innovations to market that help create competitive advantage.

1. Unifying iProcess	2. iMentors	3. iEcosystems	4. iPipe + Metrics
Common process and language used to create innovations.	Facilitators of the innovation process.	Collaboration with partners, employees, and innovators required to move innovations from idea to commercialization.	Tracking and measurement of products/services that meet the definition/criteria of innovation.

The Innovation Universe®

FRAME | GENERATE | EMBED | LEAD

GENERATING + delivering a cadence of unique + value-creating solutions for customers, while FRAMING + LEADING innovation as a core competency, EMBEDDED in every aspect of your company.

EMBED: *Company Renovation*

An ongoing, concerted effort to adapt the company so that innovation is a core competency, long-lasting and always on.

1. Change Models	2. Culture Evolution	3. Innovation Principles	4. Management Systems
Enterprise- and team-level change where change models are processes, tools, and techniques in line with innovation principles.	A system of shared assumptions, values, and beliefs that govern how people behave in organizations.	Underlying factors that form the foundation of a system of beliefs that will enable an innovative organization.	The nearly invisible framework of policies, processes, and procedures used by an organization to ensure that it can fulfill all the tasks required to achieve its objectives.

LEAD: *Unleashing Human Potential*

Actuating the innovation economy within your company by practicing, demonstrating, and implementing new leadership traits that enable innovation from everywhere and everyone.

1. Network Leaders	2. Resource Creators	3. Environment Architects	4. Change + Thought Leaders
Unite constellations of people with shared passions for personal development and innovation using new ways of thinking about talent and the work environment.	Demonstrate a track record of innovation by creating a work climate that is a magnet for talent and funding.	Create a biosphere within a company to integrate people and relationships.	Change your company to become more innovative. Transcend innovation platitudes with knowledge.

Table 9.

Epilogue

I love the beginning of a good book. I enjoy seeing how the author sets the stage to introduce the story. I especially love when a gifted writer can pull me into her world in the first few chapters, even when the subject is complex or off-putting. I marvel at storytelling that finds me, the rebel holdout, and converts me to become an advocate.

I also love the middle of a book, where the story unfolds in unimaginable ways. I become engrossed in how the author constructs the narrative. I love to experience the plot twists and surprise ups and downs of the protagonist. I also like getting lost in the middle and feeling like I never want to leave.

The end of the book? I dread it. So much so that if I am reading on my tablet, I refuse to look at the page bar at the bottom to fool myself into believing that the story may last forever. It depresses me that books, like all things, need to end.

Here, the end of this book, I will admit that the innovation journey has a similar impact on me.

At the beginning of innovation, anything is possible. We share the excitement of new ideas with fellow practitioners and conspire to create something from nothing. We collaborate in teams to ideate around new tools, to take a vague space and try to add new order to it. The beginning is where we start to see things through the customers' eyes. It is where we can allow our imagination to run amok and think differently to solve problems that no one has ever solved. It is also where we start to see that innovation is not only an intellectual quest; it is a human one.

The middle of innovation is intense and exhilarating. I share my love of the middle with countless practitioners who engage in the heavy lifting of trial-and-error attempts to make things better. It is in the middle where you can either let switchbacks derail you or turn them into positive stepping-stones to get to the next level. The middle will test your resolve. You will have your lowest lows (and possibly your highest highs) right here. Practitioners who are lifelong learners love the middle. It is where self-doubt turns to confidence. I've learned a great deal from the middle and continue to identify new insights every day.

The middle also offers unique challenges for companies. It is in the middle that companies learn that there is nothing like innovation for organic growth and employee engagement. When companies begin their innovation initiative, it is new and exciting, but that doesn't last. It's in the middle where they have to balance the checkbook and reality starts to knock. In the middle, companies either decide to change to allow innovation to work, or they become a one-hit innovation wonder.

Most companies learn that the middle demands a slow and steady pace, a constancy of purpose and patience while encouraging fast and lean innovations.

Even in innovation, I hate endings. However, it was in my last chapter as a practitioner that I could look back and not only make sense of innovation within companies, but also describe it to new practitioners. Just in this last chapter, I could see innovation clearly enough to begin to map it. I started to collect insights and to develop the Innovation Universe framework so that other practitioners could leap-frog my experience. Maybe I really do like endings, as long as they begin new journeys?

Even though I created the Innovation Universe in my last chapter as a practitioner, the Innovation Universe is only the beginning. As more and more practitioners are exposed to the Innovation Universe and use it, it morphs and expands to keep up with an innovation space that is moving at the speed of light. The Innovation Universe is a living framework.

Welcome to the Innovation Universe. I hope your journey is as rich and rewarding as mine continues to be.

Epilogue

Notes

1 The Innovation Universe is a registered trademark.

2 Michelle Burton, "8 Book Recommendations for MBAs by Top Business Schools," Online MBA Report, November 13, 2017, https://www.onlinembareport.com/articles/8-book-recommendations-mbas-top-business-schools.

3 I will refer to Whirlpool Corporation as Whirlpool in the remainder of this book.

4 http://helios.gsfc.nasa.gov (accessed October 1, 2018).

5 C. K. Prahalad and Gary Hamel, "The Core Competence of the Corporation," Harvard Business Review, May–June 1990.

6 Ronald Heifetz and Marty Linsky, "A Survival Guide for Leaders," Harvard Business Review, June 2002.

7 "PwC's Innovation Benchmark Report," PwC, https://www.pwc.com/us/en/services/consulting/innovation-benchmark-findings.html (accessed October 1, 2018).

8 Robert S. Kaplan and David P. Norton, "Having Trouble with Your Strategy? Then Map It," Harvard Business Review, September 1, 2000.

9 Andrea F. Hill, "Sustaining Growth with the Three Horizons Model for Innovation," Medium.com, https://medium.com/frameplay/planning-for-future-growth-with-the-three-horizons-model-for-innovation-18ab29086ede (accessed October 1, 2018).

10 Mehrdad Baghai et al., The Alchemy of Growth: Practical Insights for Building the Enduring Enterprise (New York: Basic Books, 2000).

11 "Ten Types of Innovation: The Discipline of Building Breakthroughs," Doblin, https://www.doblin.com/ten-types (accessed November 1, 2018).

12 "INSPIRED CHEF Trademark Information," Trademarkia.com, https://www.trademarkia.com/inspired-chef-78024707.html (accessed November 1, 2018).

13 KitchenAid is a registered trademark of Whirlpool Corporation.

[14] The Unifying Innovation Methodology (UIM) is a copyright of the University of Notre Dame, Beacon Healthy Systems, and Whirlpool Corporation.

[15] Source: Based on "Untangling Innovation Metrics: A Special Section by Innovation Leader 2015," Innovation Leader, https://www.innovationleader.com/2015-metrics-report/ (accessed November 1, 2018), and James P. Andrew, "Measuring Innovation, 2007: A BCG Senior Management Survey," BCG, https://www.bcg.com/documents/file15066.pdf (accessed November 1, 2018).

[16] Jan W. Rivkin et al., "Change at Whirlpool Corporation (A, B, & C)," Case 705-462, Supplement 705-463, and Supplement to 705-462 (Boston: Harvard Business School, April 2005).

[17] Based on Robert E. Quinn and John Rohrbaugh, "A Spatial Model of Effectiveness Criteria: Towards a Competing Values Approach to Organizational Analysis," Management Science 29, no. 3 (March 1983): 363–377, and Kim S. Cameron and Robert E. Quinn, Diagnosing and Changing Organizational Culture Based on the Competing Values Framework, 3rd ed. (San Francisco: Jossey-Bass, 2011).

[18] "About the Organizational Culture Assessment Instrument (OCAI)," OCAI Online, https://www.ocai-online.com/about-the-Organizational-Culture-Assessment-Instrument-OCAI (accessed November 1, 2018).

[19] Henri Fayol, translated by Constance Storrs, General and Industrial Management, (Martino Fine Books, 2013).

[20] Peter F. Drucker, Management, rev. ed. (New York: Harper Business, 2008).

[21] Rivkin et al., "Change at Whirlpool Corporation. (A, B, & C)."

[22] Joseph Campbell, The Hero with a Thousand Faces, 3rd ed. (Novato, CA: New World Library, 2008).

[23] Gary Hamel and Michele Zanini, "The End of Bureaucracy," Harvard Business Review, November–December 2018.

[24] https://www.pechakucha.org (accessed September 15, 2018).

[25] Tony Wittkowski, "Whirlpool Group Cultivates Creativity in the Community," Herald Palladium, November 25, 2017, https://www.heraldpalladium.com/news/local/whirlpool-group-cultivates-creativity-in-the-community/article_504b8c1d-c74b-54a2-8af5-1c6812cd76ad.html (accessed November 7, 2018).

[26] Harriet Rubin, "Art of Darkness," Fast Company, https://www.fastcompany.com/35547/art-darkness (accessed Nov 8, 2018).

[27] Jack Canfield with Janet Switzer, The Success Principles™: How to Get from Where You Are to Where You Want to Be (New York: William Morrow Paperbacks, 2006).

[28] Linda A. Hill et al., "Collective Genius," Harvard Business Review, June 2014.

[29] Stewart D. Friedman, "Be a Better Leader, Have a Richer Life," Harvard Business Review, April 2008.

[30] I was surprised to learn as I was researching this section that "Yes, and " has its own Wikipedia page: https://en.wikipedia.org/wiki/Yes,_and (accessed November 8, 2018).

[31] Erik H. Erikson, Childhood and Society (New York: W.W. Norton, 1985).

[32] Phil Newbold, CEO emeritus of Beacon Health Systems, and his innovation team conceived of Innovisits, Mike Wagner, "Bringing Outside Innovations into Health Care," Harvard Business Review, October 28, 2013.

[33] "Root Learning Map® Experience," Root, https://www.root-inc.com/disruptive-methods/root-learning-map/ (accessed November 8, 2018). Learning Map is a registered trademark of Root Inc.

About the Author

Dr. Nancy Tennant is a consultant, professor and best-selling author in innovation, leadership and organization change. She is one of the world's leading pioneers and practitioners in transforming businesses to achieve innovation from everyone and everywhere.

Businessweek named Dr. Tennant one of the 25 Innovation Champions in the world. She is an instructor at the University of Chicago Booth School of Business where she is also on the Advisory Group of the Harry L. Davis Center for Leadership, an incubator for new perspectives on leadership; and at The University of Notre Dame Mendoza College of Business where she co-founded the top-rated Certified Innovation Mentor, I-Mentor Boot Camp and Leading Innovation Workshops. She is a frequent public speaker to "C" level audiences around the world.

Dr. Tennant is the Chief Innovation Officer Emeritus for Whirlpool Corporation where she reported to two Chairmen and CEOs for over 17 years; transforming Whirlpool into an innovation powerhouse resulting in acclaim from publications such as Fast Company and Fortune while creating billions in new revenue from innovation. Dr. Tennant was also responsible for leadership development, core competencies, and organization growth. She co-founded Whirlpool University, with an enrollment of over 17,000 students per year from 170 countries.

She is the co-author of numerous articles including, The 5 Requirements of a Truly Innovative Company with Professor Gary Hamel. She is the co-author of three best-selling books: Unleashing Innovation; Mastering Virtual Teams and Strategic Innovation. She published the visual-podcast e-learning modules: Innovation Universe Master Class Series, https://innovation-universe-series.thinkific.com.

Dr. Tennant holds a doctorate from The George Washington University. She is the President Emeritus of The First Tee of Benton Harbor, a not-for-profit organization that offers life skills to at-risk youth. She is an artist, writer, poet, and aspiring ukulele player.